SEXUAL
HARASSMENT

A Practical Guide to the Law, Your Rights, and
Your Options for Taking Action

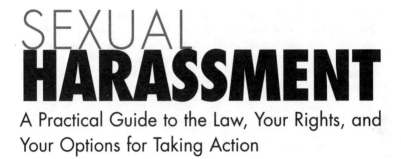

Tracy O'Shea and Jane LaLonde

ST. MARTIN'S GRIFFIN ☙ NEW YORK

SEXUAL HARASSMENT. Copyright © 1998 by Tracy O'Shea and Jane LaLonde. All rights reserved. Printed in the United States of America. No part of this book may be used or reproduced in any manner whatsoever without written permission except in the case of brief quotations embodied in critical articles or reviews. For information, address St. Martin's Press, 175 Fifth Avenue, New York, N.Y. 10010.

Jane LaLonde is a pseudonym.

Design by Nancy Resnick

Library of Congress Cataloging-in-Publication Data

O'Shea, Tracy.
    Sexual harassment : a practical guide to the law, your rights, and your options for taking action / Tracy O'Shea and Jane LaLonde.
       p.   cm.
    Includes index.
    ISBN 0-312-19524-9
    1. Sexual harassment—Law and legislation—United States—Popular works.   2. Sexual harassment—Popular works.   I. LaLonde, Jane.
II. Title.
KF3467.Z9083   1998
344.7301'4133—dc21   98-21654
                                                       CIP

First St. Martin's Griffin Edition: October 1998

10 9 8 7 6 5 4 3 2 1

To anyone who has need of this book: May you be wiser, maintain your sense of perspective, and know you are not alone in this difficult time.

To my family and friends, I am eternally grateful for your love and unwavering support.—Jane

To my family and my fiancé, thank you for your love and support. Without your understanding and encouragement, I would have been unable to come as far as I have.—Tracy

CONTENTS

PREFACE

Barry leaned over the desk and said, "You know, you make me so hot." Unsure if she had heard correctly, Jen just stared back at him. Perhaps because he didn't receive a response, Barry edged closer to her and said, "It'd be much easier to work with you if you were wearing nothing but a garter belt."

Later the same day, while Jen was making a presentation to her co-workers, Barry interrupted and said, "What does she know? She's just a girl!" Furious, Jen snapped, "Hey, if you don't pay attention, it's your problem. I'm only going over this once." To the amusement of their co-workers, Barry said, "I'm trying to pay attention, honey. It's just that when you wear that blouse I have trouble concentrating on work."

Upset and uncomfortable, Jen decided to discuss the matter with her boss. His response was that perhaps she said something, wore something, or did something to lead Barry on.

For the next several weeks, Jen wore little or no makeup, ultraconservative clothing, and went out of her way to avoid Barry. Despite her efforts, Jen faced a barrage of sexual comments every day. Further talks with her boss accomplished *nothing. Eventually, going to work became such a painful experience that Jen quit her job.*

While the preceding scenario is fiction, thousands of encounters like it take place every day. This is just one of the many forms that sexual harassment can take. Some stories are blatant, some very subtle. But even though the details vary, sexual harassment is always illegal.

INTRODUCTION

OUR STORIES

Only by his action can a man make (himself/his life) whole ... You are responsible for what you have done and the people whom you have influenced. In the end it is only the work that counts.

Margaret Bourke-White, notes, ca. 1965, in Vicki Goldberg, *Margaret Bourke-White: A Biography,* 1986

On June 8, 1995, Jane and I met for the first time. Although our fathers had been friends for over thirty years, circumstances and geography had always prevented us from getting together. On this particular evening, Jane was in my hometown for a corporate seminar. Knowing she was upset about a problem at work, her father called and asked my father to check on her. Even though the last thing Jane wanted to do was chat with her dad's friend, my father took his friend's request to heart and insisted that she come over for dinner. Meanwhile, I was having my own problems at work and was in no mood to meet anyone—let alone the daughter of Dad's old friend. The two of us, having no real choice in the matter, sat and made small talk for several hours until I excused myself to leave. My father rushed after me and told me that I should spend more time getting to know Jane. I liked her, but I was under a lot of pressure at work and just couldn't face up to being sociable. Sensing my reluctance, my father told me that we had a lot in common—we were both being sexually harassed at work.

Stunned, I went back and told Jane that I, too, was being sexually harassed at work. I apologized for not being very good company, but I was meeting with Human Resources personnel the following morning to review my complaint. Shocked, Jane told me that she had a telephone appointment with her company's Human Resources representative the following morning to review *her* complaint.

That one evening impacted both of us a great deal. Suddenly we were not alone—we had a support system. As we talked, we realized that although the details of our situations differed, there were startling similarities in the paths that our employers had taken. However, the most striking coincidence was that the emotions we experienced along the way were identical. Due to our chance meeting, not only were we relieved of the sense of isolation, but we also finally had proof that our feelings were normal based on the circumstances. Before exploring why we have made the decision to relive one of the most painful episodes of our lives by sharing what we've learned, we'd like to relate our personal stories to you. Unfortunately, if you have ever experienced sexual harassment, some of the details of these stories will probably sound familiar.

Jane

He was a serial offender . . . a blatant one at that. With him it wasn't about sex; it was power that turned him on. He was a "more valuable resource" and therefore protected by the bank. I was treated as an outsider and penalized for following their rules—even though the bank agreed that I had been sexually harassed.

My situation has been resolved amicably and another firm currently employs me. What is striking to me is how painful it still is to talk about what happened. Although my firm conducted an internal investigation and found that I was sexually harassed, I was forced to resign because of the retaliation I suffered as a consequence of reporting the abuse.

For three and a half years I worked for a large bank. I had been an outstanding employee, winning two awards for exemplary job performance. I was working in the bank's New York City headquarters when I was transferred to a regional office to assist with a complicated project. Impressed with my performance, the bank offered me a permanent position in that office.

Soon after I was transferred, I was given my own relationships to manage. I reported to Dan. He was clearly unhappy that a young woman with an M.B.A. was moving up the corporate ladder so quickly, and sought every opportunity to derail me. He was upset that so many women were being promoted to management levels and openly made comments such as "It's a man's job to make money and a woman's job to spend it." Dan felt that women who spent time on their careers were somehow "defective." He never missed a chance to whistle at me, corner me in the file room and make lewd sexist jokes, tell me I needed a man in my bed, or make comments about my body in front of others. This behavior undermined my authority and was particularly humiliating when done in the presence of my male peers. My response to these remarks was to tell him that they were inappropriate, walk away without a word, or tell him I was going to record these conversations. And as if this weren't enough of a warning, other men in the office would make comments to him such as "What are you trying to do? Get brought up on sexual harassment charges?" Dan would just laugh in response; he knew that his behavior was unwelcome, but he refused to stop.

At the time I knew his behavior upset me, leaving me unable to concentrate on my work and affecting my feelings of self-worth, but I had no idea that it was sexual harassment per se. I was familiar with the concept of quid pro quo, the sex-for-a-job type of sexual harassment, but knew nothing about the concept of a hostile work environment and how it could psychologically harm me.

Dan's behavior became more and more frequent and made me so uncomfortable that I turned to the company's corporate policy book for advice. In the brochure on sexual harassment, it outlined what constituted harassment and stated that any unwelcome behavior was wrong, it would not be tolerated, and offenders would be dealt with harshly. Based on this, I determined that I was being sexually harassed. According to the bank's written sexual harassment policy, my next step was to inform my office manager, who would then alert Human Resources.

I reported Dan's behavior to the office manager, Brian. Instead of being surprised, Brian responded by saying, "When will Dan learn?" and "Dan is prone to errors in judgment." With each complaint I made, the harassment increased—Dan seemed somehow encouraged and would step up his verbal assault. Maybe he thrived on the negative attention. While I had followed the company's procedures on sexual harassment (I had reported the situation three times), Brian hadn't. Instead of reporting it to Human Resources as required by the company policy, Brian protected Dan by keeping the situation quiet. Coincidentally, Dan happened to handle the largest and most profitable portfolio in the office.

As my situation continued to worsen, and with no one responding to my pleas for help, I became increasingly despondent. I felt absolutely powerless and quickly fell into a deep depression caused by my perceived loss of control. I had lost control of the future of my career and couldn't do anything to eliminate the pain and sense of loss in my life. Due to the daily humiliation, I lost weight, wasn't sleeping, and was tormented by thoughts of having to travel with this man (which I was required to do on a regular basis). Over time the pain and depression became so intense that I knew I couldn't deal with the situation alone. Terrified that I was headed for a breakdown, I swallowed what I had wrongly perceived as the shame of having to seek help and went to see a psychiatrist. Even though I had been able to handle other problems in my life alone, this one was too close to me to bear all by myself.

Over the course of my therapy, I was able to see that I was not to blame for the harassment. I realized that working smarter, harder, and faster would not make the abuse stop. The therapy helped me to see that I was not the one with the problem or defect—Dan was. He was saddled with feelings of inferiority, and I was merely an object in his path.

My feelings of hopelessness turned to anger toward Dan when I recognized the emotional havoc his actions had caused in my life. Once my feelings changed, I was energized by the idea that I would seek justice and confront the situation head-on. I knew that it would not be easy, but the fear of dealing with the system was much less than enduring the pain of doing nothing and continuing to live with the abuse.

From the start I had intuitively felt that I wasn't the only one Dan had sexually harassed—I had done nothing to encourage the behavior, and it just seemed too natural and comfortable to him, almost second nature. It wasn't until the other people in the office began noticing how Dan was treating me that I began hearing comments that other women had encountered similar "problems" with him.

As things in the office were getting worse, and seeing no resolution in sight, I decided to handle things myself. One morning, at my wits' end, I called Human Resources about an unrelated issue. While talking to a Human Resources representative, I "innocently" asked if I could look at a co-worker's personnel file. I explained that I was having difficulty with someone and wanted to see if anyone else had encountered the same problem before me. I was reaching out and was desperately seeking affirmation that I wasn't "too sensitive" or imagining the harassment. I wanted to believe, I *needed* to believe, that my suspicions were right, that this was a pattern and that Dan was a serial offender. The Human Resources representative said that personnel records were confidential, but asked if I'd like to talk about the situation. I declined, but secretly hoped that I had alerted them to a problem.

The next morning the head of Personnel called to ask me if I'd like to talk about my "problem." I asked him if he had heard anything from Brian. He hadn't. Before I had a chance to say anything specific, he asked if my problem concerned Dan. Shocked, I told him that he should talk to Brian first (as indicated by the company's policy) and then I would speak to him about it.

Immediately following this conversation, the bank began an internal investigation which lasted almost six weeks, during which they put me on a temporary leave of absence, while Dan was permitted to stay. I was mortified to find out that they told my clients that I had chosen to take a "personal leave of absence"—as if the situation weren't horrific enough, now my clients and peers in the industry were left thinking that I had emotional problems. This was one of the most difficult times of my life, knowing that while I was forced to sit at home, the fate of my career was being decided—and I had no say in the matter.

To my surprise, I received many calls of encouragement from colleagues—people in my office as well as people who had worked with Dan in other offices. Each caller commended me on my courage in standing up to Dan and questioned why he was allowed to continue this obviously destructive behavior. Through these calls, I also received evidence that he was a serial offender: not only had many women who worked with him quit or refused to work in the office where he was based, but the bank had settled with another employee who had accused Dan of sexually harassing her. Surprisingly, besides a feeling of relief that my intuition and claims were valid, I was overwhelmed by anger. I was furious that no one had warned me about Dan so perhaps I could have made other career decisions and avoided this situation.

During this period I combed libraries and bookstores and read everything that I could possibly get my hands on that related to sexual harassment. I have always been a resourceful person, but throughout this situation I was unable to find anything that gave me a clear understanding of what to expect from a legal and psychological standpoint. The information was so fragmented, and the need for an up-to-date cohesive reference manual so great, it became obvious that only someone who had experienced this process firsthand would be able to direct another through the legal and emotional maze. Because the information out there was so disjointed, I was unable to locate something to give me a tangible, realistic idea of what to expect in the process.

Of the information I did find, most of it was either outdated, full of legal terminology, or only discussed quid pro quo situations. In my reading I stumbled across a chapter in an obscure book that dealt with hostile-environment claims. Recognizing my situation in these words, I broke down and began to cry— I wasn't alone. It was about this time that I met Tracy and was finally able to put a face besides my own on the situation. We promised each other that we would help each other through our respective situations, and then we would help others in the same predicament by creating a "safety net" of information so they could learn from our experiences.

At the conclusion of its investigation, the bank found in my favor, giving me a letter stating that Dan had sexually harassed me. Instead of firing Dan, they then gave me the choice of staying in the same office with him or returning to corporate head-quarters in New York to an equivalent position. It defied logic that Dan was allowed to continue working as if nothing had happened, while I was given no other alternatives. There was no way I could return to the regional office without assurance that the harasser would be terminated. It was an extremely small regional office, and I was frightened of Dan's volatile temper. I didn't even want to see him after the investigation, let alone work in the office next to his. That left me the sole option of returning to New York; the option of returning to a career that would ultimately be crippled by my refusal to remain silent about the abuse and opening myself up to the very real possibility of retaliation.

For over three years I gave the bank my best; I was loyal and hardworking. But now they betrayed me. Despite their written statement that sexual harassment would not be tolerated and that anyone who engages in harassing behavior would have to face serious consequences, because his portfolio was more profitable than mine (his was larger), Dan remained un-scathed. I was the one who was uprooted from my home and friends, moved halfway across the country, and barred from seeing my clients. I was the one whose life was in turmoil; Dan's life proceeded as if nothing had happened.

I had never fully understood the concept of retaliation until I returned to New York. I was under the impression that because the bank found in my favor, I had won. I had been ex-onerated. Not even in my worst nightmare could I have envisioned what happened next: Instead of receiving a comparable position in New York (as promised), I was moved into an area I had no interest or prior experience in, and one where I would have no client contact. I made it clear from the start that I was extremely displeased with the job, but they offered me no other alternative. It was very clear that the bank did not want me to have any contact with "their" clients. Suddenly I was an outsider—and treated as such. This was confusing. The bank found in my favor. I had been wronged by one of their employees—one who had a history of this type of behavior. How could they punish me? Why wasn't Dan punished? Why was I the one forced to leave my home and a job I loved?

Deciding that enough was enough, I made the decision to hire an attorney. I had never dealt with an attorney on a personal basis before and was unsure how to go about choosing one. I had no idea what it would cost, didn't understand the nuances of contingencies and retainers, and was confused about how the monetary caps the Equal Employment Opportunity Commission (EEOC) had placed on such cases applied to my situation. I didn't know anything about the legal precedent and process and how they applied to a sexual harassment claim—and this frightened me. Fortunately, in an attempt of self-preservation, I had kept detailed notes during the torment and had left an excellent paper trail, complete with dates, direct quotes, responses, and witnesses. It became obvious to me that Human Resources wasn't there to protect me, they were there to protect the bank. I went on to file a claim with the EEOC.

My case never made it to court. For me it turned into a cost-benefit analysis: the potential length of litigation (up to four years), the monetary cost ($60,000–$100,000), and the unpredictability of the outcome dissuaded me from continuing the fight.

As difficult as the situation was, I don't regret my decision to step forward and report the harassment. I do, however, wish there had been better information available that would have enabled me to be more *proactive,* instead of *reactive,* which is the position I was forced into. I know that many victims before me internalized the abuse and felt it was easier to quit and to walk away from rewarding careers, but I couldn't do that—I had to stand up for what I felt was right.

Tracy

He admitted his behavior . . . but even with his confession, my manager refused to believe what had happened. Although I was shocked by the harasser's inappropriate actions, the most traumatic part of the ordeal was my employer's reaction.

There was a time when I thought of myself as too smart, too professional, and too capable to end up in a situation like this. I figured that if I was ever sexually harassed, I'd just tell the guy to stop and he would. And if that didn't work, Human Resources would handle it. End of problem. I couldn't have been more wrong.

For me the battle is not yet over. Although the harasser was fired over a year ago, I sought legal counsel because my employer retaliated against me. Whereas I once had a promising career at this company, my future is now uncertain: I'm treated like an outsider, gossiped about, and told conflicting stories about my career path.

Wayne was an expert in his particular field and was hired as a consultant. Starting at our initial meeting and continuing until the time he was fired, Wayne would make graphic sexual comments to me and about me. Complaints to my boss went nowhere; I was asked to "put up with it." I tried to ignore Wayne's remarks, but he humiliated me in front of my co-workers and considered me a mere decoration. No matter what I said, he'd either put me down because of my gender or twist it into a crude sexual remark.

Things progressed from bad to worse. Wayne undermined me to such an extent that my co-workers no longer listened to me—they turned to him for directions. I had lost control of my work environment.

One afternoon, Wayne made an inappropriate sexual remark

that I immediately reported to my boss, Adam. He agreed that Wayne's behavior was unprofessional but felt that I was taking it too seriously. When Adam spoke to Wayne about the situation, Wayne said he was just joking.

When I expressed my reluctance to continue working with Wayne, Adam reassigned my responsibilities to a colleague.

The next few days passed in a confusing haze. I was unhappy that my responsibilities were being taken away, and Adam was unhappy that I was causing a "problem." Adam accused me of being hysterical and suggested that I seek professional help. Despite the fact that Wayne never denied his behavior, I felt like Adam believed that I was either misinterpreting the remarks or fabricating the entire situation. And if that wasn't the case, then I must have led Wayne on—I did something, wore something, or said something that encouraged him.

I was shocked. As if Wayne's behavior weren't bad enough, now it seemed like my own boss was blaming me for the situation. Wayne's comments were hurtful, upsetting, and ate away at my self-esteem, but Adam's comments made me feel worse. This was my supervisor—someone I had worked with for quite a while, someone I liked, someone I respected, someone I trusted. And now I was made to feel like it was my fault. I started to question myself—maybe I was somehow to blame for this. Perhaps I wasn't as smart or as talented as I thought; perhaps this job was out of my league; perhaps what I thought was being nice could be interpreted as flirtatious. I became so overcome by depression and frustration that I couldn't sleep and I gained weight. The situation always weighed on my mind; I began to doubt myself so much that I lost interest in my job, my favorite activities, and socializing with friends. I was positive that I was the only one in the whole world that this was happening to, but then I met Jane. She became my lifeline. Just knowing that I wasn't alone and that my feelings were normal gave me the strength to stand up for myself.

Eventually Adam agreed to bring the situation to management's attention. I was sent to talk to a Human Resources representative. At the conclusion of this meeting, I was told that Wayne would be fired immediately and Adam would be "officially reprimanded" and made to review the corporate policy on sexual harassment. I was offered a transfer to another project, but I liked my job and believed that this was the end of the ordeal, so I said no. I expressed my fear that Adam would somehow retaliate against me, but was assured that this wouldn't happen.

Relieved that the nightmare was finally over, I returned to my office only to be called into a meeting with Eric, Adam's boss. Annoyed that I hadn't come to him first, he made it clear that he thought this issue should have stayed within the department. Eric said that he understood why Adam had said what he did; he was only trying to help me learn how to protect myself. Eric went on to say that I'm a "breathtakingly beautiful woman" and that from now on I'd have to handle situations like this by myself because I can't keep running to "big brother." I was warned not to go to Human Resources if any other issues arose; I was to come straight to him.

My previous boss, Sam, also wanted to speak with me that day. Like Eric, he was upset that management and Human Resources had gotten involved. He told me to come to him if I had any problems and that he would "decide if it's important enough to go to Human Resources with."

I had thought the nightmare was over, but now I had Eric and Sam angry with me—and these guys were high up on the corporate ladder. Not to mention that Adam was furious—and I still reported to him. With this in mind, I focused all of my energies on my job and tried to stay out of everybody's way, but tensions ran high—especially between Adam and me. Remembering Eric's request that I come to him with any problems, I asked him to have me reassigned.

A few days later, Eric informed me that I was coming to work for him. Knowing that people at his level worked almost exclusively with an assistant, I questioned what my role would be and expressed concern that this would become a clerical job. Eric scoffed at my doubts, but he also said that if I wanted to be moved away from Adam, then I had to take this position.

Over the next few months my fears were realized—I was assigned only clerical tasks. Eric even transferred his secretary and moved me into that office. Every time I requested a job description, I was told that it was "evolving." Although my title and salary remained the same, my job didn't. There were other signs of retaliation: I was the only one not assigned a mentor; I was the only one on my level to be denied business cards; and Eric even introduced me as his assistant. The Accounting Department wanted to know why my time was not being charged to a clerical budget, and despite repeated requests, it took me seven months to get a performance appraisal.

I was also the subject of gossip. Everyone wanted to know what was going on; there were stories floating around that I had screwed up so badly, they were forced to reassign me. Rumors were so rampant that Eric sent out a cryptic memo saying that I hadn't been demoted. Unfortunately, this just fueled the fire and rumors increased. Even though management was telling me that this was a great opportunity, my colleagues believed otherwise.

Months later I was eventually given my old job back. But before this move was finalized, I had to take a performance "test" to prove that I was capable of doing the job that I had done for two years before the ordeal began.

Even though the situation seemed to be resolved, the feelings of hurt and anger remained. Instead of being depressed because I no longer had any responsibility, I was depressed because I had to get up and go into the office. People were talking about me; there were questioning looks, overheard comments in the hall, and conversations that would stop dead when I walked in. I felt stuck—I hated staying, but was afraid to leave because I was worried I'd be blackballed in the industry.

As the book I worked on was wrapping up, Joan (a member of the management team) informed me that I was being moved again—and that there was a chance I'd be working for Adam. I briefly outlined the situation and told Joan that because of our history, I would prefer not to work with him. At first she seemed sympathetic, but a few days later she changed her tune and defended Adam's actions.

This encounter with Joan gave new life to the incident: suddenly I was being summoned into meetings and reprimanded for telling the truth, threatened with the size and stature of the company, told that perhaps I should ask a doctor about drugs to solve my "emotional problems," and accused of blowing the situation out of proportion. Looking back now, it becomes clearer. The company was using what Jane and I call the "fragile egg" strategy—they were using tactics to make me appear emotionally unstable, thereby nullifying my valid complaints. There were also comments from people who meant well, but hurt me nonetheless—carry ice cubes in your pockets and press them against your wrists to keep calm; in a perfect world this situation wouldn't matter, but in the real world it does; and it will keep you from getting ahead at this company.

I had thought that I was starting to come to terms with my feelings, but this resurgence of hostility and abuse shook me so badly that I got to the point where I was afraid to go to the office. I became withdrawn and spent my days trying to remain invisible. At home my life wasn't much better. With the weight of this situation constantly hanging over me, I was sad, irritable, and so very tired of life in general, all of which caused havoc with my personal relationships.

I'm not really sure what happened to change my feelings, but finally I decided that enough was enough. I had put up with a lot, but I would not have my emotional stability or integrity questioned. I had followed the corporate sexual harassment policy, but the company hadn't. Since I was in no shape to confront my employer on my own, I decided to find an attorney to protect my interests. This finally prompted the company to conduct an investigation.

I have just filed an EEOC claim and have to wait for 180 days before I can do anything else. So for the next six months I will remain here—seeing the people who questioned my ethics and capabilities and accused me of lying and being emotionally unstable. Coming to work is so stressful that on occasion I get physically ill. Some days I just want to quit; some days I'm so depressed it's a struggle to get out of bed; but on some days I'm able to pretend that none of this ever happened and can act almost happy.

I do have some support from within the company—a few people have told me they respect me for the decision to stand up for myself. While these people agree that I have been severely wronged, they don't want to publicly admit it because it could damage their careers. Others act as if I've suddenly won the lottery, but I can't emphasize this enough: Standing up for myself is in no way, shape, or form about money. I just want the situation to go away and to be able to do my job. Deciding to seek legal help was an agonizing choice to have to make; I knew it would generate a lot of hard feelings, but I felt I had to do this to preserve what was left of my self-respect and self-esteem. Regardless of the outcome, I did the right thing.

Why Share What We've Learned

Until approximately two years ago, we were two ordinary working women with definite career goals and bright futures.

We enjoyed our jobs and were excited about our prospects for advancement. Then suddenly everything changed. We encountered a situation we never thought would happen to us—we became victims of sexual harassment.

Raised to believe that the truth will prevail, that people will choose to do what's right instead of what's easiest, and to play by the rules, we both followed the guidelines set up by our employers before seeking help from the legal system. What is interesting is that although we worked in different industries and were based in different cities, our stories are very much the same.

Fortunately we had one another for emotional support, but we couldn't answer each other's questions about the process or offer one another solid advice on what our options were. This prompted us to look to books, magazines, newspapers, government agencies, on-line services, and women's groups for information on how to end the harassment. Here are some examples of what we found:

- When we asked a clerk at a major bookstore if they had any books on sexual harassment, he responded, "Do you mean adult survivors of it?"
- A title search on sexual harassment at the New York Public Library turned up only one book: *Fighting Back: Taekwondo for Women. The Ultimate Reference Guide to Preventing Sexual Harassment, Assault and Rape.* This book advocates physical violence as a response to sexual harassment in the office.
- The yellow pages listed a sexual harassment hot line. A machine answered; three messages later we are still waiting for a response.
- When we asked the head buyer of another major bookstore if they had any books written for the victim, she said no, and that since most companies had

sexual harassment policies in effect, why would anyone need such a book? We then asked, "What if the company doesn't follow the policy? Is there one book you'd recommend that offers a victim advice on what to do then?" She thought for a moment and replied that no, she knew of no such book; it had never occurred to her that a company wouldn't follow its own guidelines.

Months of searching libraries and bookstores yielded little. In more than one instance, the books the libraries had were listed as lost or stolen. In bookstores we looked at every title in the women's studies, psychology, legal reference, and business sections—and in many cases found nothing. Of the books we did find, not one provided a complete picture of sexual harassment and its effects on the victim. This was incredibly frustrating; we were victims and we needed a survival manual written for us—one that offered answers and practical advice for *surviving* sexual harassment. We wanted something written by someone who had actually experienced what we were going through, not by someone whose only knowledge of sexual harassment came from law books or secondhand stories.

After digesting all of the data we could find, we were no wiser than we were when we started. We already knew that sexual harassment is illegal, retaliation is illegal, and both should be reported to the appropriate personnel.

OK. So then what? What happens if you followed your company's published procedure for dealing with a sexual harassment grievance, and still the company does nothing? Or what if they retaliate? Can you rely on the Equal Employment Opportunity Commission or do you need a lawyer? As that public service announcement used to say, you can tell the harasser that what he is doing is sexual harassment and you don't have to take it, but then what? What if it doesn't stop? What if you get fired? What if the company makes excuses for the harasser? What happens when the company or the harasser threatens you? Or the company admits you were harassed, but just doesn't care?

There were other vital questions that went unanswered: What about the impact of prolonged harassment on your emotional and physical health? Or on your self-esteem? How do you handle the enormous pressure? Where do you turn if suddenly your co-workers avoid you or become openly hostile? How do you deal with the gossip and accusations? How will this impact your career in the future? Will you have to quit? Will you be emotionally strong enough to remain in that environment? How do you put this behind you?

Most books ignore questions such as these because they weren't written for you, the victim. They were written to educate lawyers, managers, Human Resources personnel, or psychiatrists. While we are not lawyers, psychologists, managers, or Human Resources personnel, *we are victims.* And that's how this book was born; frustrated by the lack of useful information, we promised ourselves that we would do everything in our power to help other victims by lessening the uncertainty, anxiety, and loneliness that go along with being sexually harassed. As it turned out, this project was very therapeutic for us—it gave us something positive to focus on while the negative dominated our lives.

Don't Be Discouraged

While both of our stories may make it seem as if the system failed us, the truth is that *we failed the system.* By this we mean that neither of us understood our options or how to use them effectively to protect ourselves. Human Resources personnel, corporate managers, and lawyers are aware of the rules and know how best to protect the company's interests, but the average working woman doesn't. If we had known our rights, if the information had been in front of us in black and white, we'd have been in a much better position to make intelligent, informed decisions about our futures—instead of giving the harasser and employer control of the situation and limiting ourselves to the options that they presented (which, of course, were in the company's best interests, not ours).

Having been victims, we know that it is easier to walk away from the situation than to stand up for what you know in your heart to be right. It's a frightening prospect to fight back—you are opening yourself up to the possibility of gossip, accusations, blame, threats, emotional trauma, as well as risking your career. But it *is* possible to stand up for your rights and survive. And by standing up for yourself, you don't have to march into court—there are other options. Standing up for yourself can be as basic as telling a harasser that you will not tolerate being treated in an unprofessional manner, or, as in our cases, it can mean launching an investigation and filing an EEOC claim.

There are other factors to consider: The laws are vague and rapidly changing. Sexual harassment can be difficult to prove (especially for hostile-work-environment claims), and often the employer has deep pockets, power, and time on their side, while the victim's resources are limited. Unfortunately, the EEOC can't always be relied upon for help; they have their own problems with a reduced budget, limited staff, and an exponential growth in caseload. *Victims must be their own advocates.*

Polls vary, but it is estimated that 75 to 90 percent of working women have been sexually harassed *at least once.* Here are some statistics that demonstrate how many lives are touched by sexual harassment:

- In 1994 there were 102 million women over the age of sixteen in the United States. Sixty million of these women were either employed or seeking employment in the civilian sector.[1]
- Women accounted for 46 percent of the labor force in 1994. It is estimated that women will comprise 48 percent of the labor force by 2005.[1]
- Nearly six out of every ten women (58.8 percent) were working or looking for work in 1994.[1]
- In 1994 3.3 million women held more than one job.[1]
- In 1990 there were 6,127 claims of sexual harassment filed with the Equal Employment Opportunity Commission. By 1995 this number more than doubled—rising to 15,549.[2,*]
- In just five years, monetary rewards paid out in sexual harassment claims have risen by 215 percent.[2]

Evidence shows that women are more likely to take an active role in stopping harassment if they are aware of their rights and have a greater sense of their own empowerment. And that's what you'll find inside this book: a complete explanation of your rights and the information you need to stop being victimized by sexual harassment and to initiate change.

---

[1] U.S. Department of Labor Women's Bureau. Facts on Working Women. No. 95-1, May 1995.

[2] Equal Employment Opportunity Commission. Sexual Harassment Statistics. EEOC & FEPAs (Fair Employment Practices Agencies) Combined: FY 1990-FY 1995.

*It is estimated that this number is significantly lower than the actual incidents of sexual harassment that occur. This is due to several factors: complainants are afraid to come forward; victims are unaware that what they are experiencing is sexual harassment and that it is illegal; some employers do have sexual harassment policies in place and adhere to them; and in many cases, a settlement is negotiated prior to filing with the EEOC. This number does not include harassment that occurs outside of the workplace.

We are just two people (out of many) who refused to be victims any longer. We are better off for it—today we are stronger, smarter, and able to respect ourselves for not taking the easy way out. It's difficult, but we survived. You will too.

Knowledge Is Power

The two of us are both very resourceful women, yet we were unable to locate the information we needed to understand what was happening and to retake control of our lives. If a resource such as this were available two years ago, we could have saved ourselves months of anguish by knowing we had alternatives and possibly making different choices. But at the time, we just didn't know our options.

We've learned a great deal over the last few years, most of it through our own experiences. But we've also read all of the pertinent material that we could get our hands on, thoroughly researched the latest case law, examined the Equal Employment Opportunity Commission's regulations, and reviewed the latest guidelines for Human Resources personnel. This book is not meant to be a replacement for legal or psychological advice; instead it is meant to serve as a resource guide to enable you to ask informed questions, to better deal with a lawyer or mental health professional, to prepare yourself for the battle, to give you an overview of the entire process, and to help you survive emotionally. Most important, it is meant to let you know that you are not alone and that you will be OK. We believe that we have created a comprehensive manual that will empower you and give you the knowledge and confidence to regain your life.

Victims of sexual harassment often feel limited to the three classic responses: put up with the abuse, quit the job, or sue. We've given you more options, ones that don't require you to sacrifice your career, sanity, or future. There are no easy answers, and every decision is a very personal one, but it is easier to use the system if you know how it works. That's our goal: to provide strategic direction and tactical guidelines for surviving sexual harassment. We believe this book is the most comprehensive manual about sexual harassment available today and that it gives you the tools you need to empower yourself and take back your life.

CHAPTER 1

WHAT IS SEXUAL HARASSMENT?

> *As long as you keep a person down, some part of you*
> *has to be down there to hold him down, so it means you*
> *cannot soar as you otherwise might.*
>
> Marian Anderson, Interview, CBS-TV, December 30, 1957

I struggled over the definition of sexual harassment. I knew the legal definition, but that didn't exactly translate into real life. Obviously I'm very aware of sexual harassment and am constantly searching for hidden agendas or undertones in what people say. But why is it that a single comment made by one person takes on a completely different meaning when said by someone else? How do you define perceptions? Everyone has different mind-sets and different histories that shade how they look at things. I believe it boils down to motives, what the harasser hopes to gain.—Tracy

This chapter is probably one of the most important in the book. I know when I was finally able to name what was happening to me, by finding a definition of hostile work environment in a book, subsequent to the start of my internal investigation. It was so moving that I literally started to cry when I read it. Finally, I was able to name what was happening to me. Even though I still did not know what my options were or how to handle things, at least I now knew that my reaction to my sit-

uation was normal and I was not just being hysterical. I knew that I was not alone in my feelings and found tremendous comfort in knowing that my response to the situation was not unique. I found solace in just knowing that others before me had experienced similar situations and had a similar reaction. When I read that my symptoms of depression coupled with a general disinterest in things that once made me happy were the common reaction to sexual harassment on the job, all of a sudden I experienced the clarity I needed. Unfortunately, from both a psychological and strategic perspective, I could have benefited from finding this definition much earlier; nonetheless, although I still didn't know what to do, just knowing that my reactions were normal gave me the added impetus I needed to stand up for myself, realizing full well that I might have to fight my company in my claim of sexual harassment. I found solace in learning that my reaction was much like those of other people who had experienced the same thing on the job. —Jane

In one of his books, Robert Fulghum wrote an essay discussing how a person's identity and self-worth are tied into what can be written on a two-by-three-inch business card. He goes on to discuss how often the first question people ask when they first meet is "What do you do?" It is the answer to this question that immediately forms the basis of a person's initial impression of you. When that identity is stripped away, people's impression of you changes. In fact, your own impression of yourself changes. During my experience with sexual harassment, I often thought of this essay and the simple truth behind it. That is only one of the devastating effects of sexual harassment—it takes away your very identity.

Like a fog that rolls in slowly and unnoticed until you find yourself lost in the midst of it, sexual harassment is insidious and pervasive. Besides the obvious effects—fear, discomfort in your own working environment, loss of pride in your work, to name a few—sexual harassment affects the very core of who you are as a person. Being victimized by it forces you to question yourself and to lose faith in your own judgment. This self-doubt does not confine itself to your work life; it invades your personal life as well, seeping into your relationships with friends and family. Every single comment and interaction with the harasser chips away at you slowly until suddenly one day you discover that you feel completely shattered.

Because every incident of sexual harassment is different, and because it challenges the fundamental dynamics of the male/female relationship, it is very difficult to create a precise, all-encompassing definition of sexual harassment. The legal definition does not touch upon what sexual harassment really means to a victim, and the impact it has on all aspects of her life—not just the professional. In an effort to clearly show how wide-ranging the effects of harassment really are, we have expanded upon the legal definition and created what we call the "real world" definition.

Sexual Harassment: The Legal Definition

Sexual harassment is considered a type of sex discrimination and as such is covered by Title VII of the Civil Rights Act of 1964.

The legal precedent was established in 1986 in the case *Meritor Savings Bank v. Vinson* (477 U.S.57), in which the U.S. Supreme Court ruled that harassment is sex discrimination and is therefore illegal under Title VII of the Civil Rights Act.

In regard to sexual harassment, Title VII says the following:

> Sexual harassment is legally defined as any unwelcome sexual advances or requests for sexual favors. It also includes any verbal or physical conduct of a sexual nature when the following criteria are met:

- Submission is made explicitly or implicitly a term or condition of an individual's employment;
- Submission to or rejection of such conduct by an individual is used as the basis for employment decisions affecting such individual;
- Such conduct has the purpose or effect of substantially interfering with an individual's work performance or creating an intimidating, hostile, or offensive working environment.

Sexual harassment may include physical conduct, verbal conduct, or nonverbal conduct such as sexual gestures or pornographic pictures.

Under the law, there are two basic types of sexual harassment: *quid pro quo* and *hostile environment.*

Quid Pro Quo

Latin for "something for something," *quid pro quo* harassment is the most blatant and is what most people think of when they hear the words *sexual harassment.* Quid pro quo harassment is a request for sexual favors in exchange for a promotion, a raise, or even the right to keep a current job. More succinctly, the Equal Employment Opportunity Commission (EEOC) defines it as:

Unwelcome sexual advances, requests for sexual favors, and other verbal or physical conduct of a sexual nature constitute "quid pro quo" sexual harassment when:

Submission to such conduct is made either explicitly or implicitly a term or condition of an individual's employment or submission to or rejection of such conduct by an individual is used as the basis for employment decisions affecting such individual.

Because quid pro quo harassment is usually so blatant, one incident is usually enough to support a legal claim. The classic example of quid pro quo sexual harassment is the middle-aged manager requesting sex from his pretty young secretary as a condition to retain employment.

Hostile Work Environment

Hostile-work-environment harassment is not as clear-cut as quid pro quo. With hostile-environment harassment, the victim is subjected to unwelcome sexual advances, requests for sexual favors, and other verbal or physical behavior that interferes with her work performance or creates an intimidating or offensive working environment. The main difference between hostile environment and quid pro quo is that any requests for sexual favors are not made in exchange for a raise, promotion, or as a condition for continued employment.

In an effort to clarify the definition of *hostile environment,* the EEOC created the following guidelines:

> In determining whether or not an environment is hostile, it must be determined whether or not the conduct unreasonably interfered with an individual's work performance or created an intimidating hostile or offensive working environment.
>
> The EEOC suggests that courts look at the following criteria:
> - whether the conduct was verbal, physical, or both
> - how frequently it was repeated
> - whether the conduct was hostile or patently offensive
> - whether the alleged harasser was a co-worker or a supervisor

- whether others joined in perpetrating the harassment
- whether the harassment was directed at more than one individual
- were remarks hostile and derogatory?
- did the harasser single out the charging party?
- did the charging party participate in the exchange?
- what was the relationship between the charging party and alleged harasser?

Hostile-environment claims can include many types of behavior: sexually degrading or sexually explicit comments, crude jokes or stories, leering at someone's body, displaying pornographic drawings or photographs, circulating dirty cartoons, rubbing up against someone, touching a person in an inappropriate manner, sexually based teasing, sexual favoritism, forcing an employee to put up with offensive behavior, and forcing an employee into a situation that she feels uncomfortable in.

This type of sexual harassment is much more difficult to define than quid pro quo because of the subjectivity involved; what one person may find offensive may not be offensive to someone else. *Therefore it is critical that the victim tell the harasser as early as possible that the behavior is unwelcome.* Silence on the part of the offended party may be construed as acceptance. Unless the actions of the harasser are particularly egregious, it takes more than one incident to constitute hostile-environment harassment.

The second sexual harassment case heard by the Supreme Court was in 1993. In *Harris v. Forklift Systems, Inc.,* the Supreme Court began to define what created a hostile workplace. In *Harris* the Court held that a victim of sexual harassment does not have to show that she suffered "severe psychological injury" in order to state a claim. (Until this ruling, some federal courts had been demanding the plaintiff offer proof of psychological trauma in order to validate her claim.) The Supreme Court established a two-pronged test:

1. The conduct complained of must "be severe or pervasive enough to create an objectively hostile or abusive environment that a reasonable person would find hostile or abusive."
2. The victim must "subjectively perceive the environment to be abusive."

If both of these criteria are met, there is sufficient proof of a hostile work environment.

In *Ellison v. Brady,* 924 F2d (9th Cir. 1991), the "reasonable woman" standard was developed. In this case it was determined that sexually harassing behavior must be looked at from the perspective of the victim and should be based upon the unique experience of women. The ruling states in part that "the reasonable person standard still must consider the victim's perspective and not the stereotyped notions of acceptable behavior." Since this ruling, the EEOC and the courts will look at whether the victim was subjected to behavior and conditions that any reasonable woman would consider sufficiently severe or pervasive enough to alter the conditions of employment and create an abusive working environment.

Blurred Boundaries

In an effort to develop a better understanding of sexual harassment, F. Till has expanded upon quid pro quo and hostile-environment harassment to develop a model that breaks sexual harassment into five different types. This model is helpful because it is very easy for the victim to become confused about what is and what isn't sexual harassment. Many comments that are borderline may or may not be considered harassment based upon the context of the behavior and the dynamics of the victim/harasser relationship. These clearly defined categories help to organize the victim's thoughts and solidify her perspective as to what is happening to her.

While these basic models clarify the range of sexual harassment, it is very important to note that they are not mutually exclusive, nor are they all-inclusive. It is not unusual for one case of sexual harassment to include more than one example from the model. And, of course, there are so many types of harassment that it is virtually impossible to develop a model for each. Of these five types, gender harassment is the most common.

Five Types of Sexual Harassment

Type 1: Gender Harassment	Generalized sexist remarks and behavior
Type 2: Seductive Behavior	Inappropriate and offensive (but essentially sanction-free) behavior with no penalty attached to noncompliance
Type 3: Sexual Bribery	Solicitation of sexual activity or other sex-linked behavior by promise of rewards
Type 4: Sexual Coercion	Coercion of sexual activity by threat of punishment
Type 5: Sexual Imposition or Assault	Gross sexual imposition such as touching, fondling, grabbing or assault

Sexual harassment can sometimes be ambiguous, and it is not uncommon for a victim to wonder if she is truly being harassed. There is no one-size-fits-all definition of sexual harassment that could clearly define every scenario. The difficulty with developing a concrete definition is that person A may find person B's actions objectionable, but person C does not. Here are some broad guidelines as to what is and what is not harassment:

What is Sexual Harassment	What is NOT considered Sexual Harassment
"You look like you need to get laid."	"You do not look very happy. Is everything okay?"
"That blouse really shows off your curves."	"You look nice in yellow."
Repeatedly asking a co-worker out once she's made it clear that she's not interested.	Asking a co-worker out on a date.
Your boss telling you your bonus is dependent on accompanying him to an out-of-town conference and that you do not need your own hotel room.	Your boss requesting your presence at a company dinner.
If the person repeatedly finds opportunities to brush up against you; if it is no longer accidental but deliberate.	Co-worker accidentally brushes up against you.
Sexually explicit jokes, e-mails, or faxes sent to your attention.	An isolated incident of an innocent "blue" joke making its way around the office, not directed at anyone specifically.

The Real-World Definition of Sexual Harassment

OK, so you know the legal definition of sexual harassment. Unlike most other civil wrongs, the situation isn't over when the case is settled. The ramifications can remain with you for the rest of your life. Sexual harassment can have many far-reaching effects, such as a loss of self-esteem and paranoia. When we were being victimized, we both suffered devastating bouts of self-examination. We'd constantly ask questions such as: Am I crazy? Did I imagine this? Am I overreacting? Am I doing something wrong? Could I be doing something differently? If this is sexual harassment and other people witness it, why aren't they doing anything about it?

Having experienced sexual harassment firsthand, we know that it means different things to different people. While the law does a fair job of setting the parameters as to what will and will not be tolerated, we found it helpful and reassuring to put down our thoughts as to what sexual harassment means to us.

Defining Sexual Harassment from a Victim's Perspective

To the victim, sexual harassment is a traumatic experience that undermines self-esteem and builds paranoia. Other words associated with this definition are *humiliation* and *degradation*. After experiencing sexual harassment, we developed our own definition:

To the victim, sexual harassment is very real and has many varied meanings:

- worrying about what other co-workers think about me and this situation

- worrying that I will be blamed
- being afraid people will think less of me for letting this happen
- second-guessing myself—what did I wear, what did I say, how did I act?
- questioning my own sensitivity to this situation
- questioning my own emotional stability
- staying awake at night wondering how to deal with the situation
- no longer deriving a sense of pleasure from my work
- having to let go of something I've worked so hard to achieve
- a terrible loss of self-esteem due to my inability to control things at work
- the real possibility of destroying either my career or my sense of self-worth
- having to confront a corporation I always thought was there to protect me
- the possibility of litigating with a corporation with resources beyond mine
- reliving every moment of interaction and wondering how I could have avoided it
- physical problems, such as anxiety attacks, insomnia, weight loss or gain, depression, dizziness, cold sweats, and stomach pain
- watching over your shoulder at all times
- being afraid and not really knowing why
- a pervasive fear of seeing this person
- being embarrassed and humiliated by the situation
- being lonely because no one really seems to understand
- not being free to do the work I was hired to do without a confrontation

- having someone making comments about my physical attributes
- being thrown off balance by having my attention taken off of a business situation and focusing it on my appearance
- feeling weak and alone
- finding out it that the situation doesn't disappear if you work harder, smarter, or faster

Sexual harassment is:

- a loss of identity and purpose
- a loss of self
- loss of your livelihood—even if you are not fired outright, you are no longer allowed to do your job without being hassled
- synonymous with shame and fear
- loss of hope for the future
- not about romance, a relationship, or physical pleasure
- about power

Sexual harassment can steal your goals and ambitions. Instead of being driven and excited about prospects for the future, just surviving through the day can be torture. Many women have left much-loved careers and decided that maybe they just were not meant to work in a particular industry or job. Many women, under the intense stress of sexual harassment, give up and come to believe that they do not have any control over their work environment and are powerless to end the abuse. We know that sexual harassment *does* have a great impact on your life. We also hope that by knowing what your options are, you will realize you are not alone, that you can safeguard yourself and your career and ultimately benefit from our experiences, and in the process manage to protect your:

- self-esteem
- career
- mental and physical health
- personal relationships
- energy
- right to do your job
- sense of security
- sense of power
- life as you know it
- hope for the future

Common Feelings and Responses

Some of the worst side effects of sexual harassment are the self-doubt and despair over the perceived lack of control over the situation. This lack of control, coupled with little factual information on how to remedy the situation, can destroy your self-esteem and often leads to depression. Some common characteristics of depression include a lack of hope and a general loss of pleasure in things that once brought you great joy.

It is typical, while undergoing sexual harassment, to cease caring about anything. We know from personal experience that sexual harassment is such an overwhelming energy drain that just dealing with simple tasks like getting up in the morning can pose an enormously difficult challenge. Things as innocuous as crossing the street or making a phone call can become difficult. You lose confidence in your abilities and question your own judgment in even the simplest situations. As a result, you sink deeper and deeper into yourself, until you are completely isolated from your own life and numb to what is happening around you.

While these feelings and thoughts are not unusual, it is recommended that you seek professional guidance. Talk to a trusted friend, family member, psychiatrist, or other health care professional. Getting professional help is nothing to be embarrassed or ashamed about; nor is it a reflection on the strength of your character. In most instances, it will not harm your legal rights. In fact, when building a case, it may be important to show that you sought professional help, especially when seeking punitive damages for intentional infliction of emotional distress. *Note: This book is not meant to be a substitute for professional counseling. If you are experiencing thoughts or feelings of suicide or bodily harm, seek professional help immediately. It can save your life. The longer you wait, the longer it may take to repair the psychological damage that has been done.*

We have compiled some of the emotions and situations that we encountered. You may experience some or all of them, or even others that we missed.

Psychological/Emotional Effects

Depression and Anxiety	Overwhelming amorphous sadness
	Inability to concentrate or focus on tasks at hand
	Absence of joy in life
	Panic attacks
	Insomnia
	Cold sweats
	Trouble catching your breath

Loss of Confidence/Self-Esteem	Question your actions Second-guess yourself for even minor decisions Question your abilities, talents Lose confidence in your own abilities and in the organization Try to downplay your appearance, change your hair, makeup, clothing Wonder if you are sending subliminal signals or if you are confusing friendliness with flirting Feeling that you and/or your contributions to the organization are insignificant
Embarrassment/Shame	Feel damaged for losing control Believe yourself damaged for seeking help Perceive yourself at fault for the situation; feel as if you somehow brought the situation on yourself
Fear	Fear of seeing the harasser Alarm at seeing others who are party to your case Dread of going to work Apprehension of telling your story Fear of what will happen to you, your career, your life.

Change in Personality	Social relationships falter Overwhelming sense of failure Post-traumatic stress disorder No longer enjoy socializing, hobbies, activities Lose trustfulness, become suspicious of people Insecurity Confusion
Withdrawal	Withdraw into yourself to escape the pain of the situation Belief that if you do not talk about the situation, it will just go away Disassociation from reality Distancing from work, friends, activities you used to enjoy Denial of what is happening

Physical/Somatic Effects

Gastrointestinal	Stomach pains, diarrhea, constipation Lack of appetite, increased appetite
Neurological	Insomnia, headaches, lethargy, nightmares
Dermatological	Rashes, acne, skin eruptions, hair loss

Psychological	Depression requiring anti-depressants; anxiety requiring tranquilizers
Miscellaneous	Sexual dysfunction, phobias, panic attacks

Professional Outcomes

Short-term Professional Outcomes	Career destroyed; Derails you from fast-track career
	Lose confidence in the organization
	Become unproductive; can't concentrate on tasks at hand
	Feel that if you can't handle this "silly" situation at work, you definitely can't handle "larger" projects
	Contributions are deemed worthless and unimportant
	Situation may cause a barrier between you and your peers
	Fear that your situation will be discovered by others in your company or industry
	Anger at putting in years of hard work for nothing

Long-term Professional Outcomes	May become backballed within your chosen field Loss of reputation within the industry Accused may be in position within the industry to destroy your career Could handicap you in view of others, peers Stigma attached to sexual harassment will follow you Lose confidence in your ability Situation may cause a barrier between you and your peers

CHAPTER 2

WHO IS AFFECTED BY SEXUAL HARASSMENT?

*If you think equality is the goal . . . your standards are
too low.*

Feminist Slogan, ca. 1970

By some estimates, sexual harassment affects between 40
and 60 percent of working women. Between the two of us, we
can count nine victims among our close circle of friends—and
we are just average working women. Of these friends, they
vary in age from twenty-eight to forty-four, have vastly different
professions, and can be considered very attractive to average-
looking. Some are thin and some are heavy; some are single and
some are married.

As for offenders, the notion of the middle-aged male executive as the stereotypical harasser no longer holds true. Harassers can be any age and either gender.

The difficulty of developing a template description of a typical victim of sexual harassment or a typical offender is that
there really is no typical victim or harasser. Every incident of
sexual harassment is different. Victims can be women or men;
harassers can be men or women. Victims aren't necessarily rel-
egated to male-dominated professions, nor are they limited to

traditionally female-dominated low-level positions. Attractive young women are not the only victims; middle-aged executive men are not the only offenders.

Despite this, there are broad generalizations that can be made about the typical victims and offenders. Drawing on research and data available from the Equal Employment Opportunity Commission (EEOC), the National Organization for Women, 9 to 5: The National Association of Working Women, and the National Council for Research on Working Women, we developed the following data points on who typical victims and harassers may be.

Portrait of a Victim: Can It Happen to You?

We remember watching Anita Hill testify during the Clarence Thomas hearings and wondering how this woman could allow herself to become embroiled in such a situation. We would have heated discussions with friends over the validity of her testimony; and it was easy to be of the opinion that while what she said rang true, she *let* it happen.

This is not to say that she encouraged it; rather, she did not do anything to stop it. And we simply couldn't understand that—she seemed smart, capable, and tough. At that time it was hard to imagine that we'd ever be caught in a situation like that; we were too smart.

Now we realize that it was ego and/or ignorance that prevented us from really understanding what Anita Hill was telling the American public: *Anyone can be a victim.* You don't have to look a certain way, be a certain age, or work in a certain industry. Intelligence has absolutely nothing to do with victimization. Nor do experience and business sense.

Even though evidence suggests that there is no commonality in the way victims look, the way they dress, their age, or their behavioral patterns, one or more of the following criteria apply to the majority of victims:

- Young
- Not married or divorced
- Member of a racial or ethnic minority
- Works in a male-dominated profession
- Works in an environment with an unequal male-to-female ratio
- Appears to be vulnerable and more easily intimidated
- Gives the impression of being completely dependent on her job
- Holds an unusual job, which would be difficult to find elsewhere
- Holds a high-stress position in which emotions run high (doctor, lawyer, etc.)
- Holds a position in which the corporate structure places her in a position of subservience to someone who is prone to harassing or discriminatory behavior

According to the American Psychological Association, research shows that incidents of sexual harassment are not caused by women who initiate sexual activity in hopes of advancing their careers. In addition, they estimate that fewer than 1 percent of sexual harassment complaints are false. And of the many women who have valid complaints, most do not take any action. Typically, the more educated a woman is, the more likely she is to report the situation.

Special Situations

An issue of gender

Throughout this book we refer to offenders as "he" or "him" and victims as "she" or "her." This in no way precludes the possibility of same-sex harassment or women harassing men.

According to 9 to 5: The National Association of Working Women,*

> 90 percent of sexual harassment cases involve men harassing women
>
> 9 percent are same-sex harassment
>
> 1 percent are women harassing men

When the victim is not the target

An interesting point is that according to the EEOC, *the victim is not exclusively the subject of the harassing behavior.* What this means is that the victim can be anyone negatively affected by the offensive behavior.

One example of this type of harassment is the following scenario:

> Fred, a male manager, routinely harasses Betty, his administrative assistant, by making lewd and derogatory comments about her clothing and her gender. He also asks questions about her sex life and feels no compunction about telling her about his sex life. Betty feels uncomfortable because of this behavior, yet she has not done anything to stop Fred from continuing.

*The 9 to 5 Guide to Combating Sexual Harassment, by Ellen Bravo and Ellen Cassidy, page 67.

Mary, another administrative assistant whose desk is near Betty's, overhears all of Fred's abusive behavior. She is made to feel uncomfortable and anxious; she is concerned that eventually Fred will turn his attention to her. This level of stress interferes with her ability to do her job. Eventually it is Mary, and not Betty, who files a claim of sexual harassment against Fred.

In this situation, the EEOC recognizes and protects Mary's right to work in an environment free of sexual harassment. Although Mary is not the person who is the actual target of the harasser, she is being affected by the behavior and it is affecting her work performance. Therefore, Mary has the legal right to pursue action against Fred.

Sexual favoritism

Sexual favoritism is also considered sexual harassment because it can interfere with one's ability to do one's job. In the first type of sexual favoritism, employees are affected by a consensual sexual relationship between a co-worker and supervisor. A typical scenario goes like this:

Pam is a new employee at a very large advertising agency. She is very young and has little experience in the industry. Susan is an older woman who has been with the agency for many years, and she is considered to be one of its top employees. David, who is responsible for assigning projects, manages both women.

Soon after Pam comes to the company, she and David begin a consensual sexual relationship. Within months Pam is receiving all of the plum assignments and given special allowances. Eventually Pam is promoted over Susan, despite her lack of experience.

In situations like the preceding, Susan can be considered a victim of sexual harassment because her knowledge and experience are being discounted. Because Susan is not David's love interest (also known as paramour interest), no matter how hard she works or how excellent her performance is, David will never consider it to be as good or as valuable as Pam's.

However, this type of harassment is very difficult to prove. It is not enough for Susan to say she should have been promoted instead of Pam because of her experience—rather, she needs the support of other women in the department. If Susan is alone in her views, then her claim of sexual harassment may be interpreted as jealousy.

The following scenario exemplifies the second type of sexual favoritism:

> Sam, the department supervisor, is assigned the task of promoting one of his employees. Instead of basing the promotion on the employee's experience or business acumen, Sam bases it on sex.
>
> Sam first approaches Michele and offers her the promotion if she has sex with him. Michele, realizing this is quid pro quo sexual harassment, refuses to have sex and tells Sam in no uncertain terms that if he ever approaches her for sex again, she will file a claim of sexual harassment.
>
> After promising Michele that he will never repeat this behavior with her again, Sam approaches Karen with the same proposition. Desperate for the added income, yet not at all interested in Sam, Karen agrees to have sex in exchange for the job.

In this situation, both Michele and Karen are victims of harassment. Michele, aware of her rights as an employee, did the right thing in telling Sam that his behavior was unwelcome. However, she can still be considered a victim because her refusal to succumb to Sam kept her out of the running for the promotion. Karen can also be considered a victim because, although she did have sex with Sam, she was made to feel that she had to do it in order to further her career.

A Portrait of a Harasser: Why Do They Exhibit Such Behavior?

It is important to realize that sexual harassment is about power, not sex. In a sexual harassment case, the harasser is using sex as a weapon to manipulate and to exert control over a victim. Harassers are very rarely looking for sexual gratification; their need is to feel superior and dominant to women. While the characteristics of harassers include all races, ages, professions, and even genders, a majority of harassers meet one or more of the following criteria:

- Male
- Exhibits prejudicial behavior against all groups but his own
- Views women as inferior or unequal
- Believes women should be submissive
- Believes women should be completely dependent on men for emotional and financial support
- Treats all women in a derogatory manner (not necessarily a sexually degrading manner)
- Is threatened by a change in the status quo

The easiest claims to prove are those in which the harasser is in a position of power over the victim, when he has a direct impact on the financial and professional development of the victim. However, there are extenuating circumstances in which the harasser does not have direct control over the victim:

A co-worker as a harasser

Because the offender is not in a position to harm the victim directly (by having control over either career path or income), the courts look at the entire situation. Victims must be able to prove that the company was aware of the situation and was given the opportunity to take action. It must also be proven that the company did not do anything to stop the harassing behavior.

A customer or client as a harasser

Again, the offender is not in a position to harm the victim financially or professionally. However, if the company knowingly and willingly places the victim in a situation in which she is open to harassing behavior, or if the company tries to force a person to grant sexual favors to someone the company wants to please, the company can be held liable.

> Tracy's situation was slightly different; it crossed the line between the harasser as a co-worker and the harasser as a client. Her harasser was a contract worker for the company and therefore could be considered a co-worker, yet because of his job responsibilities, he was perceived as being more valuable to the company, and therefore he was to be "kept happy" and treated as if he were a client.
>
> This man held no authority over her financially or professionally, yet he made her working life unbearable. Soon after the harassment began, Tracy informed her supervisor about the behavior. Nothing was done. Due to the unique nature of his job, Tracy understood that she was to "put up" with the situation. Her supervisor held the position that since Wayne would be difficult to replace, Tracy should either accept the

behavior or change her lifestyle to avoid the behavior (take vacation days whenever Wayne would be in the office, or transfer some of her responsibilities to others in order to avoid working with Wayne).

Five Types of Harassers

Harassers can be broken down into five basic types; however, they are not necessarily exclusive:

Serial Offender	A person who persists in abusive behavior despite repeated warnings and even psychological treatment. Often this harasser is so weak in character and so easily threatened by change that he views harassment as the only way to preserve the status quo.
Onetime Offender	A person who, for some reason, victimizes one person and never does it again. Perhaps it is because this one victim challenged him in a way that truly frightened him, or he received treatment and learned to handle his emotions, or he was frightened into stopping the behavior by the threat of a public sexual harassment complaint.
The He-Man	A person who feels the need to constantly prove his masculinity. Often this type of offender does this by degrading women. For this type of harasser, the only way to secure power and status is to steal it from those around him. Whereas most men build self-esteem and self-worth through their own achievements, the He-Man never truly rises from his own plateau, but pushes those around him down in order to make the gap appear wider.

The Laggard	A person who does not intend any offense, but still harbors the mind-set of earlier eras. The Laggard is often an older man who was raised in different times and was taught to treat women one way, but finds that the rules have changed. While he realizes that it is no longer acceptable to call woman "honey," "dear," or "sweetie," he slips into his old ways on occasion. Even though this behavior is often subconscious and unintentional, it can be detrimental to a woman because it colors how others in the working environment perceive her.
The Old Guard	Similar to the Laggard, an Old Guard harasser recognizes his behavior and defends it. Often this type of harasser is still having difficulty accepting that women are in the workforce (and that they are no longer exclusively relegated to traditional female jobs such as secretary). These men were raised to treat women as sex objects, love interests, or relatives, and now that the times have changed, they resent having to treat women as colleagues.

Why Do Men Harass Women?

Since every case is different, it is impossible to list every specific reason men harass women, but fear plays a large part. It can be fear of change in the status quo, fear of those who are different, fear of appearing to be "less of a man" because a woman can handle the same job. It can be fear of losing a promotion to a female or fear of having to report to a woman (and therefore appear subservient).

As discussed earlier in this chapter, women in male-dominated professions are more likely to be victims of sexual harassment than women in industries with a more equitable male-to-female ratio. Men working in a previously male-only environment view female co-workers as infiltrators among their ranks. Fearful that working with a woman will change the status quo (by making them change their behavior—no more stories of sexual conquests, no more sexually explicit posters or jokes, etc.), somehow make them appear to be less masculine (the macho status of the job changes if a woman can do it), or impact their lives in some other negative way, these men use every weapon at their disposal to drive women away. This includes embarrassing them, threatening them, and/or harassing them until they give up and go away (often by quitting their jobs). These men view this as a victory.

Several resources have indicated that the basic male/female gender dynamic plays a part in why men harass women. Men have traditionally viewed women as sexual/feminine beings: the mother/caregiver, the wife/lover, or the sister in need of protection. It was only recently that women in large numbers took on the nonsexual role of colleagues and equals. This transition to a different mind-set has proven quite difficult for many men, and while most men are able to draw the line on what behavior is and is not appropriate in the workplace, some men are unable to do so. It is these men who cannot adjust to the new role of women who end up possibly becoming harassers.

The Male Response to Sexual Harassment

Most men recognize and abhor sexual harassment, and these men treat female colleagues with the utmost respect. However, some men simply do not understand the concept of sexual harassment—because they believe that they would be flattered by sexual advances from a female in the workplace, they have difficulty comprehending why women get offended. Women take offense because, unlike men, they have been stereotyped by physical appearance and gender and they have had to overcome many barriers in order to be taken seriously as part of the workforce. (Remember the proverbial glass ceiling, equal pay for equal work?) After struggling for so long to be taken seriously, women get offended when all of that time and effort is minimized by a man who has never had to struggle with the same issues. In addition, women (who by far outnumber men as victims of sex crimes such as rape) live with the very real fear of physical assault and often view harassment as a prelude to physical violence.

Offenders offer several excuses for their behavior: She can't take a joke or she welcomed it. Harassers interpret "stop" as playing hard to get. They view persistence as part of a "chase." It is also not uncommon for offenders to accuse victims of leading them on by smiling, flirting, or simply being nice. The one commonality is that they never view their behavior as wrong.

The Victim's Rights

Victims of sexual harassment generally want one thing: to make the harassment stop. Going through the situation ourselves, we know that revenge, retribution, or retaliation was never an issue. We simply wanted to be able to go to work and do the jobs we were hired for. We wanted a safe workplace— free from intimidation and fear—where we could contribute our skills, thoughts, and insights, and where we would be treated with respect and professionalism.

Drawing from our own experiences and from the law, we have developed the following data points, which we refer to as the Bill of Rights for Working Women. If every company and every employee accepted these points as concrete examples of how to treat one another, we would be well on our way to eliminating sexual harassment in the workplace.

Bill of Rights for Working Women

As a working woman, you have the right to:

- Work in a professional environment
- Work in a place free of harassment based on gender
- Work in an environment free of sexually degrading literature, pictures, jokes, and comments
- Do the job you were hired for
- Be treated as a professional
- Be treated with respect
- Be taken seriously when lodging a complaint
- Make a complaint without fear of retaliation
- A complete and confidential investigation by a neutral party
- A swift and just resolution
- Be considered for promotions and raises on the basis of talent and performance
- Be treated in the same manner as other employees

The Harasser's Rights

In keeping with the spirit of "innocent until proven guilty," people accused of sexual harassment have the right to a fair and confidential investigation by a neutral party. Sexual harassment complaints should be handled with the utmost discretion, respect, and concern for the individual's privacy. The ramifications for all parties involved are numerous and extensive; it would truly be a tragedy for word of a complaint to get out and an innocent person's professional reputation to be destroyed before there was proof of wrongdoing.

All companies should have a clear grievance process, and only those who need to know should be informed of a pending investigation. Both the victim and harasser should be made aware of the potential legal ramifications stemming from possible libel and slander suits.

The Employer's Responsibility

The company (or employing entity) has the obligation to strictly adhere to city, state, and federal laws; to handle the situation immediately and confidentially; and to actively prevent retaliation. They are morally bound to have a neutral party investigate each complaint and offer a practical solution to the problem.

While not every state requires employers to have a sexual harassment policy, it is in every company's own best interest to implement one. Prevention is the best way for a company to protect itself, so it is also wise to implement training programs to teach employees about sexual harassment. It is also critical that employers adhere to the policies that they have in place.

CHAPTER 3

RECOURSE: YOU'VE BEEN HARASSED—NOW WHAT?

Action is the antidote to despair.

Joan Baez, *Rolling Stone*, 1983

I *followed my company's sexual harassment grievance policy to the letter and reported it on three separate occasions to the head of our office. Because my harasser was a "big producer" (he generated a lot of money for the firm), my complaints never made their way to Human Resources. I was getting no relief and knew that either the harassment had to stop or I could not continue to work. I just wanted things to be the way they were before the harassment started.*—Jane

At the initial meeting with management to inform them of the situation, the first question I was asked was "What do you want?" Without even thinking about it, my response was, "I just want it to stop." And that was true—I didn't want money, I didn't want revenge, I just wanted everything to go back to normal. I wanted to be able to do my job without the cold, gripping fear that enveloped me whenever this man was in the office. I didn't want to duck into empty offices to hide when I heard his voice down the hall. I didn't want to waste my energy on making myself invisible.—Tracy

The first step in making a harasser stop his offensive behavior is recognizing that what you are experiencing is indeed sexual harassment. Even if all of the evidence suggests that you are being sexually harassed, its often hard to believe that it's actually happening. It's a perfectly natural reaction to deny the situation—even though statistics prove that most working women have experienced some form of sexual harassment, many don't realize that they are being victimized in this way. Educate yourself about sexual harassment. Write down your experiences and compare them to the examples given in the previous chapter. You may find it helpful to talk to someone about what is going on—a trusted friend, mentor, family member, even a psychologist or psychiatrist. (At this stage, be careful of what you discuss with your co-workers. Anything you say can potentially be used against you, and you don't want to be accused of damaging someone's reputation.) Trust your gut feelings. If someone's behavior makes you uncomfortable, you do not have to put up with it. You have every right to tell the offender to stop his behavior.

If the harasser touches you or threatens you with physical violence, seek legal help immediately. It is always wise to protect yourself rather than risk violence. In cases in which he explicitly asks for sex in exchange for a promotion or job (see quid pro quo harassment on page 28), only one incident is enough to constitute a case of sexual harassment, so you may want to consider consulting a lawyer right away.

Once you determine that you are experiencing sexual harassment, the next step is to remedy the situation. There are several typical responses that may ultimately end the harassment: confronting the harasser, informing your supervisor, telling Human Resources, retaining legal counsel, or quitting your job.

Your decision is a very personal one, based upon your emotional and financial resources and taking into account hopes, dreams, and plans for the future as well as personal and professional objectives. While we cannot possibly recommend one option over another, we can outline what we have learned and let you know some of what you can expect.

Protecting Your Emotional Health

The single most important piece of advice that we can give you is to protect yourself. As a victim, you are trapped in an unhealthy situation that is not of your doing. It's natural to experience a whirlwind of conflicting emotions, including paranoia, doubt, anger, and fear. It's critical that you realize that these feelings are normal and that it's OK to seek help to deal with them.

Don't be embarrassed to seek professional help. Millions of people see professionals for all sorts of reasons. The most important thing is to protect your mental health. Often victims are so emotionally battered by the time to take action comes that they lack the intellectual clarity to realize that they need to get help. Self-esteem is low and it is a natural reaction for victims to wrongly blame themselves for causing the problem. When feeling this low, it's hard to believe that you are valuable enough and worthy enough to deserve to be treated with respect. Should you begin to slip into this trap, protect yourself by talking to a professional who is experienced in dealing with sexual harassment and discrimination cases.

The enormous stress of the situation may also take its toll on your physical health. Be sure to eat right and get plenty of rest. And don't forget to exercise; we both found that going for a run or riding the stationary bike was a great way to work off some of the aggression and anger.

There is one thing to keep in mind when seeking treatment from any doctor: Be sure to inform your health care provider that the ailment may be caused by the severe stress of the harassment. It may be vital to your case that you prove that the mental or physical problems were caused by the abuse; the only way to do this is to inform the doctor of the connection at the outset.

Don't Allow Yourself to Be Bullied

A co-worker suggested that before going to meet with management, I place an ice cube in a plastic bag inside my pocket. When I felt upset, I should put my hand in my pocket and place the ice against my wrist. It seems that she had read somewhere that pressing ice against your wrist made it physically impossible to cry. She didn't want me to get visibly upset in front of company managers. I know she meant well, but it really didn't help.—Tracy

Throughout your ordeal, you will be pulled from every direction. People will offer all sorts of advice—usually with the best of intentions, but often harmful. You will feel battered, utterly exhausted, and completely confused. It is now that you are at your most vulnerable.

Take your time when making any decision; don't let anyone push you into anything that you are not ready for. Think everything through very carefully. You may find it helpful to keep a personal journal of your thoughts and feelings (but be sure to keep it completely separate from your log of the facts).

Educate Yourself

Knowledge is power. Even if you merely suspect that you are being victimized by harassment, *obtain a written copy of the corporate sexual harassment policy and review it thoroughly as soon as possible.* It is critical that you follow this policy to the letter. In progressive companies it may put a stop to the situation. If it doesn't and your situation continues, then you may eventually need to prove in a court of law that you did make a good-faith effort to work within the corporate guidelines. Document how you followed the rules laid out by the company and how they did (or did not) work.

To further strengthen your position, do some research on sexual harassment. Familiarize yourself with your company's policy, contact the Equal Employment Opportunity Commission (EEOC) for the most current state and national laws, and get in touch with national organizations such as the National Organization for Women (NOW) and 9 to 5. Many organizations offer support groups where you can get emotional and legal support. Refer to the Resource Guide on page 177 for more information.

Know the Harasser

Most harassers do not limit their abuse to one person. Look around for signs of a pattern of harassment. Are you aware of anyone else who may be experiencing the same type of behavior? Be alert; people may drop hints about the accused's treatment of other people during the course of everyday conversations. Do you know of anyone who quit suddenly for an unknown reason? Has there been a lot of turnover in your current position? Start asking questions. Try to get any information you can. In most cases there is someone in the office who has kept in touch with the employee who has left and can offer some insight as to why she left. Be careful how you phrase the questions; be as diplomatic as possible in your quest for this extremely valuable information.

Gathering information about patterns of harassment at this stage will bolster your case later on. If you do discover other victims, it can provide an invaluable source of emotional support. You may also find it easier to go to Human Resources together. The company will be far less likely to accuse you of lying if there is someone else to substantiate your claims.

Keep Good Records

Initially I expected the company to respond in a moral and responsible manner, so I was a bit reluctant to actually go so far as to document every detail. First, it was emotionally draining. When these incidents happened, I was often so shocked that it was a struggle to recall every detail. They happened quickly, and it hurt to relive the particulars. Second, it was time-consuming. Not having the foresight to realize that this situation would become so large and ugly, I thought that it would be a waste of time. Third, I believed that the company would take my word for what had happened. I never believed that the people I worked beside for several years would betray me by telling investigators what they thought the company wanted to hear, rather than what actually happened. For these reasons, I looked upon keeping a detailed log as a form of betrayal to the organization I worked for. Today I am thankful that I kept notes. When I was accused of lying, all I had to do was read over what I had written to reassure myself that I wasn't crazy.
—Tracy

Looking back at my situation, this is one of the most important aspects of coming out of the experience whole, and probably what I handled the best. Keeping good notes of all the details of your harassment, while it is happening, is probably your best defense in telling your story, retaining a lawyer, and settling your case. If you have the benefit of referring back to the facts that you have documented instead of just relying on your memory when emotions are running high, it allows you to be somewhat objective in the midst of turmoil. A detailed account of the situation, your harasser's reactions, witnesses' reactions, what your supervisor did when you explained what was happening, and how the Human Resource area responded will help paint a more lucid picture of the actual scenario.—Jane

No matter what course you expect the situation to take, keep a journal and save any offensive notes, e-mail, or pictures that you may have received. Keep records of any employment-related promises or threats, no matter how subtle they are. Some of the following suggestions may seem very cloak-and-dagger, and it may appear to be overkill, but you never know when you will need to prove what you say. Unfortunately, in this world of skepticism, people are reluctant to take you at your word, and you may have to prove your case to investigators. Remember, in most situations, the investigators work for the same organization that you and the harasser do—and they don't want to do anything to jeopardize their own careers.

When emotions become involved, and they always are when dealing with something as highly charged and personal as sexual harassment, it's much easier for you, the victim, to respond to stereotypical responses such as "She's just another hysterical woman" when you can counter with the cold, hard facts. Furthermore, when you can quote witnesses as to their opinion of what they've seen, the problem takes on a larger scope. Then it's not just you, it is also the witnesses who were offended by the comments and abusive behavior. And although it's very unusual, witnesses can also file a complaint of sexual harassment (see page 46 for more details).

To help you keep track of all relevant information, we've compiled a list of questions that you should ask yourself as you are recording/transcribing what happened:

- What did he say? (Use his exact words if possible.)
- What did you say?
- What date did the incident occur?
- What time did the incident occur?
- Where did the incident occur?
- How did you respond physically? (Did you step away?)
- What was the context of his comments and behavior?
- How do you know he was serious?
- Were you touched? In what way were you touched?
- What was your response to him during the incident?
- What did you say before and after?
- How did the harasser know that his actions and/or comments were unwelcome?
- What exactly did you do or say to indicate that the behavior was unwelcome?
- What were you wearing?
- What was your emotional state? How did you feel?
- How did he make you feel?
- Who was present? (Include names, titles.)
- Who may have overheard what happened? (Include names, titles.)
- Where were the witnesses in proximity to you?
- Did you speak with the witnesses regarding what they overheard and/or saw?
- What exactly did the witnesses say?

As you keep your log, you should include any documents pertaining to your job performance (there have been incidents in which a company has tried to fire an employee after she's filed a complaint), as well as any odd comments made by co-workers or supervisors, and what your emotional responses were. Don't be afraid of including too much information; if you think it may be important, write it down. It may prove to be crucial to your case.

Sample Log Entry

A good log may prove to be the crux of your case. Here is an example of the type of notes you should keep:

> **Monday, September 8, 1997, 3:48 P.M.:** I was sitting at my desk typing up notes on the Smith project. I was concentrating on my work, and was startled when suddenly I felt a hand placed on my shoulder. Looking behind me, I discovered it was Steve Jones, a senior associate with the firm.
>
> I immediately slid my chair away from him in order to remove his hand from my shoulder. Steve leaned close to me and said, "I really like that blouse. But there's a problem. I can't stop thinking about what's underneath it. Why don't you take it off and show me so I can get back to work?"
>
> I replied by saying, "That type of comment is not only inappropriate, it is offensive."
>
> Steve answered, "Can't you take a compliment? I'm just trying to be friendly."
>
> Before I had an opportunity to respond, Steve turned around and left my office. He seemed angered by my comment.
>
> I was wearing a black suit with a long-sleeved white silk blouse. It was buttoned all the way up. At the time of the incident, I had taken off my jacket and draped it over the back of my chair. Whenever I left my office, I put on the jacket and buttoned it. Sally Rogers, a secretary with the firm, walked by during the conversation. I asked her if she overheard what had happened, and she said that she had only overheard Steve's last remark. There were no other witnesses nearby.
>
> This event made me uncomfortable in my own of-

fice. Afterward I locked the door because I was afraid that he would come back. During the incident, I was fearful of what Steve would do, and while I thought it important to clearly let him know that his behavior was unwelcome, I didn't want to make him angry with me. He is a senior associate, and he does have the opportunity to keep me from being promoted.

Wednesday, September 10, 1997, 10:15 A.M.: As I walked from my office toward the break room to get a cup of coffee, Steve followed me. As I reached the break room and started to pour myself a cup of coffee, Steve blatantly leered at me—eyeing me up and down in a slow and deliberate manner. I turned away, embarrassed and disgusted. He then said, "I can picture you bringing me coffee in bed in the morning. Of course, you'd be naked." He laughed.

I responded by telling him, "You're disgusting and not behaving like a professional."

Steve said, "You're a broad. What would you know about being a professional?"

I said, "Obviously a lot more than you," and I quickly left the room.

I returned to my office shaken and upset. I was so frazzled I was unable to complete a project, and as a result, missed an important deadline. I was wearing a navy blue pantsuit with a high-collared blouse.

After going through the effort to write down all the details of what's happening, you must take appropriate care to protect your notes. One of the first questions our attorney asked was whether we were keeping notes. After we responded affirmatively, she then told us that if we were keeping our records on a company-issued calendar, notepad, or even on their computer network, it was within their rights to demand that we turn the notes over to them.

Purchase your own notebook or calendar to keep a log. Look for a bound diary or journal to which pages can't be added or removed—this makes it harder for anyone to accuse you of tampering.

Store your log in a safe place, preferably at home. Anything in your office or on your personal computer directory is legally considered to be company property; locked drawers or password-protected files will not safeguard your records. Even if you store electronic files on a floppy disk, they have a way of accidentally getting copied into other directories. There have been cases of offices being searched and notes taken; in both of our situations we believed that our computer files had been tampered with.

You may need to prove that the log entries were actually written on the dates that you claim. There are several ways to do this: Mail the pages to your home, but don't open them, so that you have the postmark to prove the dates. Or you can have them notarized. Consider mailing your notes to an attorney as they are created.

Proof of Job Performance

Another important way to protect yourself is to gather all employment records and copies of performance appraisals. Companies often try to discredit victims in the wake of a sexual harassment claim by trying to prove a weak employment record. To be on the safe side, keep any written evaluations, thank-you notes, complimentary e-mails and memos. Jot down any verbal compliments. It never hurts to prove your work history was good—especially since, if you end up leaving, the company probably won't be rushing to provide a reference.

If your direct manager or supervisor is the harasser, it is likely that he will use your job performance as a wedge to push you into accepting his advances or to fire you. Since sexual harassment is about power, harassers use this behavior in an attempt to ease their own feelings of inadequacy and inferiority, so it's not surprising that harassers who are in supervisory positions are very likely to try to blemish your track record. To harassers in this position, getting rid of the victim appears to be the easiest way of getting rid of the problem (in this case a threat to his job, status, power, reputation).

If, after the company is made aware of the issues, you are due for a performance review, be sure to do your homework. Be able to provide a specific list of your accomplishments and demonstrate how you've performed since your last review. If there is anything that you disagree with in the written review, don't hesitate to write a rebuttal.

In some cases management may be reluctant to provide a review. Since reviews are often tied into compensation changes and promotional opportunities, don't hesitate to ask for it when it's due. You may want to consider checking with Human Resources to find out the policy on reviews; perhaps there is a deadline as to when they must be completed.

Witnesses

Having witnesses to the offensive behavior will undoubtedly strengthen your case. The more people who can verify your story, the harder it will be for a harasser to deny. As soon as an incident occurs, look around for potential witnesses. Discuss the incident with the witness; ask questions to determine exactly how much was seen or overheard. Keep notes of what the witness tells you. A sad fact is that if an investigation is launched, witnesses will be reluctant to get involved, will deny what they've heard or even go so far as to lie. It will be easier to jog their memory if you have discussed the event with them and are able to provide details as to where, when, and what you spoke about. Be careful, though; you don't want to say anything that may compromise your position in the future. It's important to keep to the facts and avoid sharing any personal feelings or disclose what your intentions are. If you need to speak with someone about your feelings, consult a professional. In addition, by speaking with witnesses you may discover that you aren't the only one being victimized.

Confrontation: Telling the Harasser to Stop

When faced with harassment, it is often the best course of action to immediately inform the perpetrator that this behavior is not welcomed and found offensive. Depending upon the type of harasser you are dealing with (see chart, page 51), this may stop him in his tracks. For serial harassers, you may need to take further steps to ensure that your working environment returns to normal.

Why tell the harasser to stop? Because doing nothing is just as much of a choice as taking action. One sure way to keep the harassment alive is to ignore the behavior—silence can easily be interpreted as acceptance. Silently stewing does not alert anyone that you are unhappy; you must be vocal. The EEOC recommends that the victim *"directly inform the harasser that the behavior is unwelcome and that the victim wants it to stop."* It is important to communicate that the conduct is unwelcome, particularly when the harasser may have some reason to believe otherwise. (Consider the old saying, "Her lips say no, but her eyes say yes.") Harassment often grows from subtle comments to bold advances because the harasser mistakenly assumes that no objection is an invitation. Therefore it is very important to speak up as early as possible before things escalate and put the harasser on notice that the behavior is unwelcome, unprofessional, and will not be tolerated.

If it is not possible to speak with the harasser at the time of the incident (for example, if you are reluctant to make a scene in front of clients or guests, or you are taken off guard and miss the opportunity to speak), ask to speak with him privately. Be careful, though; don't give the wrong impression. You don't want to make it appear as if you are making a date. Treat it as if you are setting up a business meeting. Never ask to meet off premises or after business hours.

When confronting the harasser, keep the following points in mind:

Be vocal. Silence is usually interpreted as acceptance. By his very nature, any person who treats another in a negative or derogatory manner is not very intuitive. If he's unfeeling or uncaring enough not to see the pain he's inflicting, he won't understand that walking away silently is an indication that the behavior is unwelcome.

Be clear. Don't rely on thinly veiled sarcasm to get your point across. It's often lost on these men; or worse, it's interpreted as acceptance or encouragement. To ensure that your message is heard and understood, choose your words carefully and say exactly what you mean. Be blunt and direct; leave no room for misinterpretation or misunderstanding. If necessary, tell the harasser that what he is doing is sexual harassment and that it's illegal. Do not apologize—you are not in the wrong for telling him to stop a behavior that makes you feel uneasy.

Be specific. If inappropriate behavior has happened before, mention that to the harasser. Sometimes pointing out specific examples will force the harasser to notice a pattern—and make him see that you are building a case against him. Concrete examples make a more forceful impression than do sketchy allegations.

Be strong. Don't back down from a confrontation with your harasser. If someone acts in a manner that makes you feel uncomfortable in your own working environment or keeps you from doing the job you were hired to do, you have the right to tell him to stop. You do not have to take the abuse. Make him aware that you are too strong to be bullied—that you won't surrender your power to him. Don't allow him to treat this situation lightly; impress upon him the seriousness of it. Once he realizes that you won't back down, he may look elsewhere for a way to boost his own warped self-esteem.

Be calm. Telling your harasser to stop the offensive behavior will be one of the most frightening things you'll ever have to do, but it's vital that you keep your emotions in check during the confrontation. Don't cry; don't yell. If you need to express your feelings, speak to a professional.

Be professional. This is not the time to engage in a war of words. State your case, then walk away. The purpose of confronting your harasser is to tell him to stop and to inform him of what you plan to do if he doesn't. If he tries to draw you into an argument by challenging your position, disputing your facts, or denying your claims, don't try to convince him that you're right. It may be tempting to argue back—especially if he attempts to nullify your complaints by refusing to take them seriously—but losing your composure will only weaken your case.

Be yourself. Realize that this is not your fault. Don't try to alter your physical appearance, demeanor, or actions in an attempt to stop the harassment. This won't turn the harasser's attention away from you. Sexual harassment is about power—not sex. No matter how you change yourself, it won't change his behavior.

If the initial confrontation fails to deter the harasser, you may find it necessary to speak with him again. At this time consider mentioning that if he does not stop and desist, you will be forced to take further action—and don't hesitate to tell him exactly what steps you will take.

Fear of Confronting the Harasser

It's completely natural to experience some anxiety when preparing to confront anyone—let alone someone who has caused such turmoil. It isn't essential that you confront him directly; the EEOC recognizes that it is not necessary for a victim to confront a harasser in person in order to have a valid claim. While we recommend telling the harasser to cease and desist, *if you have any reason to believe that the situation may turn violent or that you are risking physical harm, do not confront the harasser.*

After the Confrontation

Once you have asked the harasser to stop his behavior, the harasser may take your warning to heart and stop harassing you. If this happens, don't dwell on the harassment. Instead, take extra care to keep your relationship on a strictly professional level.

Sometimes the harasser will view your complaints as insignificant and he will continue on as if nothing ever happened. To get his attention and to make him take you seriously, you may need to consider taking the confrontation a step further by writing him a letter (see the following section).

In other cases, the harasser will be angry and/or scared and will try to extricate himself from the situation by doing anything in his power to "make it go away." A common way of doing this is by threatening the victim with some sort of retaliation—a countersuit, charges of defamation of character, even the loss of employment.

These threats are often knee-jerk reactions, a desperate attempt on the part of the harasser to wrest control of the situation away from the victim. By standing up to the harasser and telling him that this behavior is unacceptable, the victim is regaining control over the situation and reshifting the balance of power. Uncomfortable by the changing power of dynamics in the relationship, the harasser will make an attempt to grab the power back.

Knowing why the threats are made doesn't make them any easier to hear. The key is not to panic. Think about the situation calmly and rationally—and if it helps, confide in a trusted friend, family member, or therapist. Often the threats are just the harasser blowing off steam.

However, it is wise to keep track of any conversation you have with the harasser. Be sure to write the incident down in as much detail as possible in your log.

Writing a Letter

If telling the harasser to stop doesn't work, you may want to consider sending a letter; he may take it more seriously than a verbal remark. Tell the harasser exactly why you are writing and clearly outline specific incidents. Then let him know exactly what you expect him to do—to cease the behavior—and what course of action you plan to take if he doesn't stop. Depending upon your situation, you may want to make a copy for your supervisor, his supervisor, or Human Resources.

To ensure that the letter is received, send it certified mail. Don't hand-deliver it; not only won't you have proof of receipt, but you may be inviting a confrontation. It's usually better to give the harasser time to digest the letter; chances are, he'll seek you out to either offer an apology or to vent his anger.

Sample Letter to a Harasser

The National Organization for Women offers this sample letter:*

Joe Smith, Senior Accountant
Jones and Company
222 Elm Street
Anywhere, USA 12320

Mr. Smith,

I am writing this letter to inform you that I do not welcome and have been made to feel **(uncomfortable) (intimidated) (angered)** by your action**(s)**. This **(These)** action**(s)** I am referring to is **(include):**

List specific incidents of harassing behavior with dates and offending statements made by the harasser.

This behavior is offensive to me and constitutes sexual harassment. This **(These)** incident**(s)** has **(have)** created a **(an) (unprofessional) (tense) (stressful) (detrimental) (harmful)** working environment that interferes with my job performance, particularly in any matter that requires contact with you. Therefore I am asking you to stop this illegal harassment now.

---

*Source: National Organization for Women.

Optional Paragraph: If you continue with this behavior, or harass me further as result of this letter, I will deliver a copy of this letter **to (your supervisor, _____) (the Personnel Department) (my union representative) (the president of the company, _____).** *(Note: this contact is dependent upon the employer's grievance procedure, if any exists.)* If necessary, I will file a formal complaint with the **(Equal Employment Opportunity Commission) (state or local Fair Employment Practices Agency),** which investigates charges of employment discrimination.

Sincerely,

Jane Doe

(cc: _____)
(Encl.)

Note: Be sure to make copies of your letter. Also be cognizant of any in-company grievance procedures that may give you an opportunity to rectify the situation before pursuing legal action.

CHAPTER 4

INTERVENTION: WHERE TO FIND HELP IF THE HARASSMENT DOESN'T END

You must do the things you think you cannot do.
Eleanor Roosevelt, *You Learn By Living,* 1960.

Unfortunately, in most cases, simply telling the harasser to his face to stop the abusive behavior will not make it go away. Most harassers have been given plenty of warning signs before the situation deteriorates to the point at which a confrontation takes place; warning signs that, for whatever reason, they have chosen to ignore. It's also hard to believe that in this day and age, with stories of Anita Hill, Bob Packwood, and Paula Jones in the newspapers and splashed across the TV screen, harassers have no inkling that their behavior is offensive, illegal, and just plain mean. For these reasons, it's not unusual for victims to reach a point at which they must answer a very difficult question: What do I do now?

If you ask victims in the thick of their situations what they want to see happen, most would likely say that they just want the harassment to stop. Victims generally don't want money, vengeance, or fifteen minutes of fame; most want their lives to go back to normal. Contrary to what the media would have you believe, suing for damages in a sexual harassment case is neither an easy or painless way to get ahead. Rather, it is a long, drawn-out process in which every aspect of your personal life is open to examination. Therefore it is important that victims give their next step careful consideration.

Typically victims have three options: do nothing, quit your job, or report the harassment. Deciding which road to choose is a very personal choice. While it's very easy for outsiders to rush to judgment as to what should be done, they have no way of understanding the anguish and pain that accompanies the choice, nor do they have to live with the consequences of the outcome. Whatever you choose to do must be the right decision for you, and you must be prepared to see it through to the end.

Take a Breather

Be very careful not to rush into hasty decisions. Waiting a few days before setting things in motion can be beneficial—it will give you time to collect your thoughts, make plans, think through options.

When in an emotionally charged state, it's easy to rush to action. Take a few days to yourself before doing anything. Time has a way of helping shift everything into focus, and it's never a good idea to make critical decisions when in such an emotional state. It may be tempting to run into your boss's office and yell, "I quit"; we certainly felt like doing that on more than one occasion. But you must think about your long-term goals, and how any choice can impact your career, personal life, finances, and emotional health. You may consider consulting a professional in order to crystallize your thoughts; sometimes talking things out with a trusted adviser will help steel your resolve.

One caveat: While in the short term, waiting before determining a course of action gives you time to think, waiting too long can be harmful (as there are statutes of limitation governing how long after the incident you can report sexual harassment). Once you have formulated your decision and developed a plan, follow through with it quickly and efficiently.

Taking No Action

Looking back on the course of my case today, I believe that I waited too long before taking action. I was paralyzed with fear—I was scared of the consequences of any decision, let alone the wrong one, so I waited several months before seeking legal help. Knowing what I do now, it's clear to see how my case would have been much stronger and easier to prove had I acted in a more timely manner.—Tracy

When faced with difficult decisions, there is always the option of doing nothing. Doing nothing is just as much of a decision as taking specific action. You may not feel comfortable filing a formal complaint, yet you feel that you can't quit your job due to financial or other constraints, so you may be tempted to wait and hope that the situation will abate. Don't fool yourself—doing nothing almost always leads to nothing changing.

At first you may believe it easier to simply live with the behavior, but it will take its toll. Remaining in the situation without any sort of intervention can be devastating. By this time it's likely that the harasser is aware that you are uncomfortable. The harassment can escalate because the harasser may view you as making empty threats and he'll feel more secure in his own position. This type of systematic abuse eats away at your self-esteem, and over time you'll discover that all of the joy that you once derived from your career will be gone. Not responding to the problem will not make it go away. He will not simply get bored and frustrated by your lack of response and give up. In fact, often the opposite happens. Harassers need to push victims down in order to build themselves up, so the less you say or do, the weaker you become and the stronger he becomes.

Note: In almost every case of sexual harassment, taking no action can also be considered a choice. There are virtually no cases in which the options of quitting or speaking out are stolen from the victim. Never is there a situation about which you can do nothing.

If you are unable to quit your job and there is no one within the company to turn to for help, contact one of the organizations listed in the back of this book. They can provide advice, support, and in some cases, even legal help.

Quitting Your Job

Deciding whether to quit your job is difficult. On one hand it's very easy to recommend walking out; it definitely ends the abuse. On the other, the anger and disgust surrounding sexual harassment make it just as easy to recommend fighting back and proving to the harasser that he can't get away with such behavior.

This decision is far more complex than it appears on the surface. No matter what choice is made, a lot of baggage goes along with it, so before jumping into any decision, carefully consider your entire situation and the impact that your action will have on your life. While every situation and every life is different, here are some commonalities that may help you in your decision:

Positive aspects. Leaving the company will end the harassment because effectively it lifts you out of the middle of the storm. Some women find this option the most attractive; the abuse is ended, there is no "public outing" of the situation, and there is no long and ugly battle.

Negative aspects. Leaving your job without taking action to end the harassment provides no sense of closure. You may feel as if the harasser "won." You may be walking away from a career that you have worked very hard for. It might prove difficult to find another job at the same level with the same potential. You may even be confronted with the possibility of having to change careers.

If, after thinking things through carefully, you feel this option is right for you, then do it. It's OK to quit. Quitting is not acquiescing, nor is it a sign of failure. You need to carefully consider your life and what is right for you. Fighting back takes a lot of time and energy, and depending on the company you work for, their sexual harassment policy and history of handling this type of situation, it may be in your own best interest to switch jobs. No amount of money, no amount of prestige, no job—and by this time any semblance of a career has been stripped away by the harassment—is worth risking your mental and physical health. ***Note: If there is any possibility of physical danger, do not hesitate to quit your job. Seek help immediately.***

Follow the Corporate Sexual Harassment Policy

Regardless of how silly the company's sexual harassment policy may seem, it is important to follow it closely. Try working within the confines of the policy—should the case ever go to court, you'll be glad that you did. Victims of sexual harassment often lack confidence in the mechanism to allow them to voice their complaints. This is understandable—how can a system comprised of people aligned with the organization be completely objective about that organization? Especially if one of the people involved is a friend or longtime associate?

It is this company mechanism for settling harassment disputes that is the first step in the formal grievance process for most victims. Whereas some organizations deal with sexual harassment swiftly and fairly, there are still some companies that are either naive about sexual harassment and simply do not know how to handle it, or make a decision to "not rock the boat" and protect the harasser. If the case is not handled quickly as soon as it is brought to the attention of management, then chances are that the company has reasons to either fear or protect the accused. The harasser may be considered "more valuable" by earning more money for the organization, being more senior, or having strong allies within the organization.

Most of the people involved in the grievance process are members of the Human Resources Department—and the Human Resources Department is the company's first line of defense against attack. Think about it. It is their job to protect the company financially by examining insurance claims, they protect the company from legal action by creating the criteria for hiring and firing staff, and they are the ones who develop the rules for keeping employees in line. If their job is to protect the company from its own employees, why should employees think that Human Resources will protect them from retaliation by the corporate entity?

In addition to being intimidating, the mechanism simply cannot work because it is based on flawed logic. The Human Resources Department's primary goal is dealing with the sexual harassment issue. It may not always work in the best interest of the victim; therefore it is crucially important for the victim to know her rights and to protect herself when dealing with the company's grievance procedure. The program designed to deal with the problem is controlled by the company, and the company is usually your adversary (especially once the situation has gone this far).

Reporting the Harassment

Reporting the behavior is the scariest and most challenging option. For us, although we did briefly consider taking no action or quitting, we almost instantly rejected them as possibilities simply because we felt that they were inappropriate for us. Without some sense of closure, we wouldn't be able to face ourselves. To us, fighting back was the only decision that we could live with. Remember, what was right for us may not necessarily be right for you. Choosing to quit your job does not nullify your particular ordeal, weaken your claims, or invalidate the pain and suffering you have gone through. All it does is remove you from an intolerable situation in the manner that is least disruptive to your life and healthiest for your emotional well-being.

There are many reasons why women don't report sexual harassment, the most compelling of which is that women who do report it are often retaliated against. It is one of the most patently unfair aspects of sexual harassment: you are victimized, so you follow the rules to seek justice, then you are victimized again for following the rules. This is enough to keep women from helping themselves and ending the abuse. Why on earth would someone want to suffer twice? Wouldn't it be much easier to just walk away from it? As if that weren't enough of a reason not to report the behavior, getting the company involved by doing so makes it public.

Yes, reporting the harassment will mark you—regardless of what the company claims, of what the Equal Employment Opportunity Commission (EEOC) promises, it will follow you throughout your corporate history. But it will give you a sense of empowerment. It gives you the opportunity to do something to regain control over your life. It is usually your one chance to fight to reclaim your life instead of letting someone else's actions determine your fate.

Although every situation is different, and every company is different, there are some commonalities in the pros and cons of taking action. You can probably add several to the list, but here are some that we discovered as we were going through our individual cases.

Positive Aspects of Taking Action

Empowerment. Any time you stand up for yourself, you are telling the world that you deserve as much respect and consideration as anyone else. Even if you think that the company policy won't protect you, you'll feel better for doing something to end the harassment. Taking a proactive stance toward putting an end to it will give you a sense of empowerment—a sense of reclaiming your life.

Control. Taking action (any action) and making decisions (any decisions) provides an inherent sense of control. In most sexual harassment situations, the sense of control is one of the first things stolen from the victim; so grabbing it back is particularly gratifying.

Awareness. Bringing your situation to the company's attention will raise a flag that indicates that they need to reevaluate their harassment policy or provide more and/or better training.

Assistance. By reporting your harasser's behavior, you will initiate an investigation. This will ultimately lead to some sort of disciplinary action or psychological treatment, which will teach him that the behavior is unacceptable and won't be tolerated.

Set an example. Harassers rarely target only one victim. By taking a stand against him, you may encourage others to come forward. By being open with the situation, you can help others to realize what harassment is and that they don't have to take it.

Respect. People always respect those who stand up for what is right—especially when it's fighting for justice in the face of intolerance.

Strength. There is a sense of strength that goes along with fighting for what's right. At times you may feel like David taking on Goliath—that right beats might.

It feels good. A sense of pride always accompanies actions that you believe to be right. And by doing something, there is a sense of accomplishment—a sense of taking control over the situation. Being your own person and taking a proactive attitude toward your life feels great.

Negative Feelings Associated with Taking Action

We'd be remiss if we didn't tell you that there are some risks to taking action. When experiencing sexual harassment, you will go through myriad emotions—and often they will be contradictory. Feelings don't always make sense, but it may help you to know that you aren't alone in what you are thinking. We doubted ourselves often, even though deep down we knew that what we were doing was right. Here are some the emotions we felt:

Weakness. The mere thought of standing up to an entire organization is overwhelming. There were times over the course of our cases that we felt we couldn't continue with the battle; this is common. But fortunately this is just the downside of a turning wheel of emotion—one day you feel strong and ready to take on the world, the next you feel fragile and delicate. It takes a little time, but the wheel never stops turning and soon you will be back on the upside.

Confusion. We were bombarded by advice from co-workers, family, and friends. The harasser and the company probably tried to distort the facts, and we began to second-guess ourselves. If you become too tense to think straight, take a break. Go for a walk, isolate yourself for a few hours, take a nap. Get a fresh perspective on things. Refer to your log to remind yourself of the facts, and listen to your instincts. Lots of people are willing to give advice, but most really can't understand what is happening to you because they have never experienced it firsthand.

Fear. Sometimes the fear and stress became so overwhelming that we were tempted to just run and hide from the situation. It's OK to feel that way; everyone does. Look at the situation—who wouldn't be terrified? Just remember that you have the truth on your side.

Hostility from co-workers. There was always someone who didn't believe our claims. The harassers had support systems within the organization as well. They had friends, too. And these people sided with him. There were also those who resented us for "rocking the boat." These people were usually frightened—they didn't understand sexual harassment and were afraid that if they spoke to us, we would accuse them. Other people felt that we were overreacting—or that this type of behavior is just something women have to deal with.

Hostility from employers. Our companies didn't automatically believe us; instead they took many steps to discredit us.

Lies. Harassers often lie to protect themselves.

Blame. Many companies believe that any claim of sexual harassment reflects poorly on them. Our companies focused the blame on us, suggesting that we were the catalysts—that somehow we initiated the harassment. The company will almost certainly look for anything that will damage the victim's credibility and herefore nullify any claims.

Intrusion. In sexual harassment cases, your personal life can be opened up to examination. There have been cases in which judges made victims prove that they hadn't dressed provocatively by forcing them to bring their clothes to court. They can ask very personal questions about your social life. In addition, companies will not hesitate to dig up any evidence that can help them, no matter whether it's relevant.

Exhaustion. Lodging a formal complaint of sexual harassment is a long and arduous process. Sexual harassment is a complex issue, and as such, there is a lot of legal wrangling that surrounds it. Harassment cases are not settled quickly; rather, it can take months or even years before there is a resolution.

Pain. Even though we knew in our hearts that we were fighting for what is morally and ethically right, it was terrifying to take on a corporate entity. Co-workers whom we considered friends no longer spoke to us; we were excluded from work-related social activities and suddenly found ourselves outcasts. We also felt embarrassed by the mere fact that we were embroiled in this type of situation.

The purpose of disclosing the pros and cons is not to intimidate you or stop you from doing what you believe is right; rather, it's to enable you to make an informed decision. Sexual harassment is always ugly and it's impossible to escape unscathed. But hopefully, knowing what typically happens to others who have been victimized will provide some comfort and enable you to fortify your position. Remember, you're not alone, and the situation you are facing is not unique.

Taking the First Step

If you make the decision to turn to the company for help, be sure to thoroughly review their sexual harassment policy prior to contacting them. As mentioned in an earlier chapter, one of the first things you should do when encountering a case of sexual harassment is to obtain a copy of your company's policy and study it thoroughly. It's critical that you follow it to the letter; at some companies the policy may in fact stop the situation. If it doesn't and your case progresses along, you may need to prove to a court that you did adhere to the company's policy.

If you feel comfortable speaking openly and honestly with your supervisor, you may choose to discuss it with him or her before contacting Human Resources. If you and the harasser report to the same person, then reporting it to your manager may be enough to stop the situation.

Remember, although the company may make a good-faith effort to keep the situation confidential (they usually have more of an interest in keeping it quiet than you do), word will probably leak out. No matter how strong the confidentiality clauses in the corporate harassment policy are, it is impossible to guarantee that no one will overhear a remark, get a glance at a confidential memo, or even be apprised of the situation by a friend involved in the incident. Once you make the company aware of the harassment, the situation seems to take on a life of its own. Be ready for this to go public and try to prepare yourself accordingly.

Making a Complaint

An informal complaint differs from a formal one in that instead of jumping into the pool, you are only dipping a toe into the water. Usually a first step, an informal complaint can be a brief conversation with your supervisor, asking about the situation "hypothetically." Or it can be sitting down with a manager and detailing every incident. It is referred to as an "informal" complaint only because this type of intervention does not usually include launching an investigation and there are no lawyers involved. It is more of a fact-finding mission, a test to see how the company will react.

Determining whom to speak to first may be tricky. Look for a sympathetic manager or mentor whom you trust. If the harasser is your immediate supervisor, speak with his boss or another manager.

Sometimes the situation ends here. The manager may speak to the harasser or reassign one of you. Or he or she may act as a mediator and try to resolve the situation by speaking with the two of you. However, if there is disciplinary action involved, the situation may require that you follow the formal procedure.

In more formal situations you may be required to sit down with a high-level manager or someone from Human Resources to discuss how the incident will be handled. Typically, before anything happens, an investigation into the incident is launched, but it really depends on the company's sexual harassment policy.

The Investigation Begins: What to Expect

My company put me on a leave of absence while they conducted the investigation. They told my clients that I was on a "personal leave of absence." The investigation dragged on for six weeks while I had no idea if I would be able to continue with my career. I don't know what hurt more—the sexual harassment or the alienation I felt when the leave of absence began. —Jane

My company launched an investigation only after I got a lawyer. They refused to allow me to have my attorney present during the actual questioning.

The company's view was that this was an "internal" matter and that it would be "inappropriate" to have an "outsider" present. Actually, their attitude clearly demonstrated that they were angry with me for getting a lawyer involved at all. Because of this squabbling over whether I could have legal representation during the investigation, I believe that I was viewed negatively by the investigators before they even met me. —Tracy

The investigation is a formal inquiry into what happened. It is the opportunity for neutral parties to sit down with the victim, the harasser, and witnesses, and interrogate them. Based upon what they learn, the investigators will make a recommendation to the company as to what they believe took place and as to what should be done to rectify the situation.

Ideally investigations will take place soon after the initial complaint. The investigators should be trained in sexual harassment and have experience in this type of issue. They should also be completely independent of anyone directly involved in the situation and should be as unbiased and objective as possible. In some cases the company hires outside consultants to come in and conduct the investigation; in others the investigators are members of the Human Resources Department.

As negative as this may seem, it must be acknowledged that whether the investigators are employees of the company or hired by the company, *they have an alliance to the organization.* Whereas freelance consultants are more likely to view the case objectively, no one depending upon the organization for a paycheck is going to be anxious to inform them that they have a real problem that they may be liable for. Companies want the situations to disappear—they generally don't want to spend the time or money to implement formal training. And firing the harasser is never a simple option—there is always the possibility of a countersuit. All of this is important to you because you need to realize that this will be an uphill battle, and that you are starting with a disadvantage.

At the onset of the investigation, you will probably receive written confirmation of the time and location of the questioning, and who will be present. If the company is planning on having several people there, and you would rather speak one on one with the investigator, tell them that. They may grant your request.

Before the date of the initial meeting, practice going over what you will say with a trusted friend or family member. Get your thoughts organized, and refresh your memory by reviewing your log. The investigators may try and trip you up on the facts, so be sure to go over them before the meeting. Important: Do not bring any notes with you to the meeting. You need to be able to tell the story in your own words. The investigators will be more likely to take you seriously if you can speak from memory. In addition, you may be tempted to hand over a copy of your log if they ask, and this may ultimately harm you if the case ever goes to court.

Have an Objective in Mind

Make sure your objectives are well thought out and in your own best interest. When asked what I wanted by my company, I said I just wanted to get away from the harasser. And after they concluded the investigation and found in my favor, the company granted my wish—they got me away from the harasser by transferring me back to New York.

Although I requested a transfer, I should have been more specific—the New York office was too closely aligned with the other office for me to be comfortable.—Jane

One of the first questions you will be asked is "What do you want?" By thinking through this issue prior to the investigation, you'll be able to offer suggestions as to what you'd like to see happen. It will also give you a chance to figure out what is in your own personal best interest: a transfer, termination package, or whatever you feel is reasonable and enables you to resume working in a professional environment.

In some cases a financial settlement with a benefits package may be the best option. If you clearly see the writing on the wall and know that you will never be treated fairly at that company again, then a package quickly removes you from the situation, saves you time and money, and provides a cushion so you can go out and find other employment. Keep in mind that it may take more time than you anticipate to secure another position.

The Questions Begin

I was a little nervous when my investigation began, but relying on my notes gave me a sense of comfort. I had the facts on my side—I was able to quote witnesses' reactions and specific details. I would not have been able to recall the details in the midst of the turmoil of the investigation had I not kept a comprehensive account of every incident.—Jane

One of the most frightening experiences of my life was walking into the conference room where the investigation was to take place. To protect myself, I was wearing my mother's guardian angel pin. I kept touching it and reminding myself how I would survive. It was deeply humiliating to relive all of the events, but I made it.—Tracy

At the very start of the interview, the investigators should outline the entire process: how the corporate policy works, what will be the next step, and what happens when they reach a conclusion. The investigators will try to make you feel at ease.

Then they'll ask you to tell them what happened, usually holding their questions until you are done.

Typical questions include:
- Where did the harassment occur?
- When did the harassment occur? When did it begin?
- If there was a time lag between the incident and the complaint, why did you wait? Why report it now?
- Did you ever tell the harasser to stop? That you were offended?
- Did you do something else to reject him?
- If not, why not?
- Were there any witnesses? If so, who? What did they see?
- What is your relationship with the witnesses?
- Do you have any notes, pictures, or other documentation supporting your claim?
- Do you know of anyone else who has an issue with the harasser?
- What do you want?
- Are you happy with your job?
- Why do you think this is sexual harassment?
- Do you get along with your co-workers?
- What is your relationship with him like?
- Have you ever had any type of social relationship with him?
- Have you ever had any type of social relationship with any other co-worker?
- Have you sought professional help to deal with your feelings?
- Have you had other psychological problems in the past?
- Have you every experienced an incident like this before?
- What was your relationship with your last employer?
- Why did you leave your last job?

Keep in mind that while the EEOC and the National Organiza-tion for Women recommend that investigators refrain from ask-ing questions that are accusatory (such as what were you wearing), some investigators do ask them. Be prepared.

During the initial meeting you may feel as if you are repeat-ing yourself over and over. And you might be—often investi-gators will try and trip you up by asking the same question in two or three different ways, looking for inconsistencies in your story. For instance, they may ask when the first incident of ha-rassment occurred, then later on they may ask how long ago the first incident occurred. They will probably also ask ques-tions that seem to have no bearing on the situation; answer them succinctly and honestly.

Anyone would be nervous in this type of setting; it's per-fectly normal and understandable. You will likely be intimi-dated and easily confused. The best way to handle this is to tell the truth. Chances are that prior to the discussion they will have obtained your personnel file and have reviewed your cor-porate history, so any falsehood on your part will be known. Don't embellish; try to stick with the facts and avoid going into detail about the emotional aspects.

Take your time answering the questions. Odds are that you will forget certain details; if you remember important informa-tion after the meeting, you can always contact the investigators later. Think carefully about what you say. Don't volunteer too much information; just answer what they ask. The key is to re-main as calm as possible—above all, you don't want the inves-tigators to discount your claims and consider you a "hysterical female."

After you have told your story, they will repeat the process with the harasser and any witnesses that they choose to speak with. They may even contact co-workers who have no knowl-edge of the situation in an attempt to glean information about your habits, personalities, work styles, and even trustworthiness.

As soon as your portion of the interview is completed, re-treat to a quiet spot and write down as much detail of the interview as possible. You may never need to use it, but it may prove invaluable should there be some sort of disagreement over the outcome of the investigation.

A Conclusion Is Reached

The investigators rely on several factors to come to a conclusion: evidence given by the victim and the harasser, evidence provided by witnesses, and the credibility of those involved. When the case boils down to a "he said, she said" type of incident in which it is strictly your word against his, the investigators use their own intuition to gauge the believability of your story.

Although corporate investigators would never admit it, seniority, positions of the parties, and personalities also play a role in this. Even if you have witnesses and evidence on your side, don't be surprised if the investigators claim that no harassment took place or that it was much more limited in scope than you claim. The results are never very clear-cut; they will either admit or deny that you were victimized, but there are several directions that the outcome could take.

Keeping in mind that the role of the investigators is to objectively sort through the facts, yet most are part of the Human Resources Department and therefore have a primary function of protecting the company's interest. Don't be surprised if they agree with the facts you provided yet disagree that it was harassment and the company is liable. Here are some commonly used defenses offered by companies:

The employee welcomed the sexual advances: If an employee engages in off-color jokes or frequently talks about her sex life, the employer may claim that the plaintiff welcomed and actively participated in the friendly bantering and there was no possible way the employer could have known anything was wrong.

Failure to notify the proper department: In some cases, even if you make your immediate supervisor aware of a sexual harassment problem, if it is not brought to the attention of Human Resources or the designated point person for grievances, then the company can declare that they were not properly notified and therefore are not liable. It's critical that victims follow the sexual harassment policy.

Failure to complain: In the Anita Hill situation, many people didn't believe her story, stating that if things really happened as she told them, she would never have continued to work for Clarence Thomas and would have reported him immediately. Several court cases have confirmed that an employee's failure to verbally reject her harasser's advances did not necessarily make the conduct welcome; many times the victim gives the harasser the benefit of the doubt for as long as she can, often choosing to ignore the harassment until she can't take it anymore. Nevertheless, it is a good idea to report the harassment as soon as possible with the intent of nipping it in the bud before things progress from bad to worse.

Harassment not pervasive: In *Carrero v. New York City,* the employee's supervisor attempted to kiss and touch her five times and made several sexually offensive comments to her. The employer argued that Title VII does not make such "trivial behavior" unlawful. The court stated that a "female employee need not subject herself to an extended period of demeaning and degrading provocation before being entitled to seek the remedies provided under Title VII."

Referenced conduct not harassment: The most obvious and frequently used defense is that the conduct in question was not in fact sexual harassment. As stated before, sexual harassment is extremely subjective, but the courts have stated that the totality of the circumstances must be examined, adopting "the perspective of a reasonable person's reaction to a similar environment under essentially like or similar circumstances." Because this defense is widely used, it is important to accurately record witnesses' responses and to locate others who may have also been victimized.

The company agrees you were victimized

While I was on my leave of absence, my employer phoned me and requested that I fly to New York for the results of the investigation. To my amazement, they presented me with a letter on the bank's letterhead. It stated that they had found that I had been sexually harassed. Incredibly, in the end they treated me as though I were the harasser.—Jane

In my case, the harasser admitted his actions to my boss (although neither referred to it as sexual harassment). This, in conjunction with a host of witnesses, was enough for the company to admit that sexual harassment did in fact take place. However, they would only go so far as to acknowledge that in hindsight the complaints were handled clumsily.—Tracy

Even if the investigators conclude that you did suffer sexual harassment, that doesn't mean that your life will go back to normal. It depends on what they plan to do about the situation. Here are some possible scenarios:

The company agrees that you were harassed, but they . . .

Retaliate against you. Retaliation is a tricky concept that is discussed in detail in Chapter 7. However, since retaliation is illegal, companies will never admit to doing it. And often it is just one or two people doing it.

The company may discipline the harasser or even fire him, but other co-workers or members of management may harbor resentment toward you for instigating such an action. Either consciously or subconsciously, they begin to treat you differently. It may be snubbing you socially or passing you over for well-deserved promotions or plum assignments. Because retaliation is so insidious, it's very difficult to prove. However, keep a log of everything that happens and try to gather any evidence you can. If you can prove it, you may consider seeking legal advice, contacting a national labor organization for help and advice, or filing a claim with the EEOC.

Offer you a transfer. This option is not necessarily negative. Unless it is a transfer to another region, or to a job that is not comparable to your current one, it may be a welcome change. Although it is with the same company, you may look at it as a fresh start.

However, don't let yourself be forced to take a transfer to an undesirable location or into a job that is not what you want to do, that earns less money, or is considered a demotion.

Offer you a separation package. Again, this is not necessarily a negative option. Depending upon the package offered, you may wish to take it and start fresh somewhere else. Just make sure that the company is willing to provide complimentary references.

Lightly discipline the harasser, leaving both of you in the same environment. Giving the harasser a slap on the wrist and then expecting the two of you to continue working together as if nothing had happened is ridiculous. The harasser will be angry with you; you will be self-conscious and intimidated around him. Although the harasser has been warned not to continue (and has probably been threatened with severe disciplinary action should it continue), he cannot help but be furious. With the threat of being fired hanging over him, he most likely won't commit overt harassment, but will probably do little, unprovable things to make your life difficult. And there is always a threat of him retaliating off-premises. (Remember: should you have any reason whatsoever to fear physical harm, seek assistance immediately.)

At the very least you will be so uncomfortable around him that your productivity will decline sharply. Since the harassment has stopped (and especially if he does not exhibit any harassing behavior), you have very little basis for a formal legal complaint. You may want to consider seeking a new job to remove yourself from the situation.

Do nothing. There have been cases in which even though the company admits harassment took place, they take no disciplinary action against the harasser and do nothing to restore your working environment to a professional level. Contact the investigators and ask what they plan to do to alleviate the situation, and ask for a written response. Should no action be taken, consult an attorney. By not doing anything, the company is demonstrating their lack of consideration for you and their lack of seriousness toward the complaint.

The company says that you have not been victimized, and . . .

They fire you. Legally you cannot be fired for filing a claim of sexual harassment unless it is proven that you deliberately filed a false charge. By keeping a log over the course of several months and by taking steps such as informing the harasser directly to stop, you are underscoring the validity of your claim. Realistically, companies do whatever they want, legal or not. If you are fired without cause, talk to an attorney. You may be entitled to any lost wages and they may have to give you your job back.

They retaliate against you. Keep a log detailing every incident of retaliation and gather any evidence you can to support your claims. Retaliation is difficult to prove, but if you believe that you have been further victimized in this manner, consult an attorney.

Since the investigators say no harassment took place, the harasser wouldn't be disciplined and is most likely still in the environment. Be sure to keep track of any interaction you may have with him.

They offer you a transfer. Although the company has denied any harassment took place, by offering you a transfer they are offering you a way out of the situation. Consider it seriously, especially if you think you'll have trouble finding another job.

They expect you to continue working with the harasser. To expect to be able to have a professional working relationship with a man you have accused of sexual harassment is simply not rational. By this time he has been cleared of any abusive behavior. So not only is he angry, but he is also feeling "untouchable" because he's been cleared. This is the most dangerous situation—he feels invincible and is convinced that his behavior is normal and acceptable.

Keep track of all encounters and seek legal help. Even if a lawyer feels that you do not have enough of a basis for a case, it can't hurt to discuss the facts and get a legal opinion.

Note: Since the harasser will not be disciplined if there is no admission of victimization by the investigators, you might be expected to continue working with him. Maintain your log and keep as much distance between the two of you as possible. Should the harassment continue or escalate, seek legal counsel. If there is any chance of physical harm, seek help immediately.

CHAPTER 5

THE LEGAL ROUTE: IS IT RIGHT FOR YOU?

I did what my conscience told me to, and you can't fail when you do that.

Anita Hill, interview, "60 Minutes," CBS-TV, February 2, 1992

M*any times throughout the course of my ordeal I contemplated getting legal help. In fact, many acquaintances suggested suing. One friend in particular, uneducated about the intricacies of sexual harassment and the legalities surrounding it, kept a running tab of how much money she thought I could collect.*

I did not seek legal help in order to achieve financial gains. I knew going in that the chances of any sort of settlement were slim, and I was (and am still) convinced that no amount of money would be worth subjecting myself to a lengthy court battle.

Deciding to even contact an attorney was difficult. It was almost as if it were a point of no return—once I did this, the matter took on a whole new dimension. By having lawyers involved, it suddenly became "real" and much more serious. After all, I knew I was being victimized by sexual harassment and retaliation, but if I could convince a lawyer of the validity of my claim, then surely the company would finally take the situation seriously and do something about it.

I realized that I could no longer protect my interests by myself when I was told that Human Resources considered me a "liar" with "emotional problems."

Jane had already gotten legal representation, so I contacted her attorney. Looking back now, I realize that I should have gotten a lawyer much earlier in the process. —Tracy

When I was finally able to put a name to what was happening to me, and after I sought help through my company's internal reporting channels, I realized that I had a decision to make: resign from my job or seek legal remedy for the harassment. Fortunately, I had a close friend who happened to be a partner at a large New York law firm. When I spoke with him about my dilemma, he told me that his firm did not handle employment law out of their New York office, but he would speak to the other lawyers in the office to find the best law firm for me to contact. At the same time, I spoke to another friend whose father happened to be a labor lawyer for a large company. By sheer coincidence, both recommended that I arrange a meeting with the same firm in the city, a firm specializing in employment law.

That said, the decision to actually call the law firm and tell my story was excruciatingly difficult. For me it felt like I was exposing my situation to the "outside world." I was petrified of what it would do to all the time I had expended on my career, and frightened and confused at what bringing another party into this mess would mean, not to mention how frightened I was of the potential cost of protracted litigation. Furthermore, I didn't know if the law firm would even take me seriously and believe that I had a case. I knew lawyers were expensive and my funds were limited—in contrast to my employer's resources, which appeared unlimited. I didn't have a trust fund or wealthy family to foot the legal bill, which I had heard could easily surpass $100,000. I also knew that as shallow as my pockets were, the opposite was true of my potential adversary; the company I worked for had profits of over $1 billion in that year alone. All *this said, I knew that I could not just quit my job, as many before me had done. I was too stubborn to allow him to just get away with the harassing behavior and, in essence, win. I couldn't just cower and quit. I knew that I had to explore any and all legal options available, until I was exhausted, financially and physically. I truly knew that if I did not stand up for myself, it would be difficult to look at myself in the mirror. As painful as things were, I had to come to my own rescue for the sake of the battered remnants of my self-esteem. It was my last and only chance to attempt to gain back what I had lost, and this experience had taken so much from me already.*

After the repercussions started, people asked me why I had done what I had done. They couldn't understand why I chose to stay and fight. Many people told me that if they had been put in the same situation, they would have just walked away. I could not just walk away from everything I had worked so hard to achieve. My reply to them, which would still be the same today, was that if they had been put in the same situation, they would have done the same thing. I had no choice; it was my final act of self-preservation. —Jane

While we have experience with sexual harassment and some of the legal remedies, we are not attorneys. This chapter is meant as simply an overview of the process, not a substitute for legal advice. Since laws vary widely from state to state, you must check with the Equal Employment Opportunity Commission (EEOC) and legal representatives from your own state. We have done our best to ensure that the information provided in this book is accurate, but in today's world of rapidly changing laws, it is best to seek professional legal help.

Those who have never experienced sexual harassment like to compare the victims to lottery winners. They think all it takes is a trace of evidence and a good lawyer, and then the company will shower them with money. In reality, most victims receive little more than a basic severance package—a few months' salary—and lost wages. The big cases making headlines are usually settled before they ever see the inside of a courtroom, and these huge settlements are simply a result of publicity.

Anyone who equates sexual harassment with big payoffs has no firsthand knowledge of the subject. The potential costs, in time, energy, and money, needed to prepare for court are enormous. If you cannot negotiate an adequate settlement early on and have to press ahead to the courts, the outcome is like a roll of the dice. If, after much time and money, your case goes to trial, it is a gamble inasmuch as the jurors may look at you and see someone who "looks OK." They may think that what you were dealing with is no worse than what they deal with on a daily basis. Or you may encounter a judge who believes that sexual harassment is not a serious issue. It is truly a gamble to go to court; it is extremely expensive, time-consuming, and mentally and physically draining. However, sometimes litigation is the only choice.

It was only six years ago that the rights of victims of sexual harassment were broadened: The Civil Rights Act of 1992 provided for trial by jury in cases of sexual harassment and other job discrimination; it also permitted the awarding of damages, instead of just back wages. It was only after the Anita Hill issue that President Bush signed the previously ve-toed bill. In signing it, he capped the total amount of damages that an employee could recover in any sexual harassment case to between $50,000 and $300,000, based upon the number of people employed by the company.

Deciding Whether to Seek Legal Help

At some point during the course of any sexual harassment situation, the victim asks herself, do I really need a lawyer? The only time you don't need one is if the company views sexual harassment as a serious issue and takes a firm and proactive stance toward maintaining a discrimination-free workplace.

However, if you have made a good-faith effort to work with the company to resolve the issue and it has not been resolved to your satisfaction—in other words, the situation has not improved since your complaint—then the answer is yes. (Note: In many cases, the company's first line of defense is that they took appropriate action and promptly resolved your problem to the best of their ability. Therefore it's important that you follow the company's sexual harassment policy to the letter.)

Many states, such as California, are making it unlawful for employers or employer training programs to fail to take all reasonable steps necessary to prevent discrimination and sexual harassment. In addition, some states are mandating that firms provide sexual harassment awareness training.

There are many manuals instructing corporations on the proper way to set up a sexual harassment policy. The details, we will not discuss in this section, as we will assume that either your company does not currently have a policy or they have chosen not to follow it.

Typically it is better to speak with a lawyer as soon as you realize that the company is not going to defuse the issue. Simply having an initial consultation does not mean that you have to follow through with legal action; rather, it will provide an objective view of your particular situation and fully inform you of your options. Most lawyers charge a consultation fee, so ask how much it is when you call to make an appointment.

As strange as it sounds, if you do have a valid legal claim, the point at which it will be necessary to actively involve a lawyer depends upon the size of the company you work for. If you work for a company that employs *fewer* than fifteen people, you should contact a lawyer to help you evaluate the appropriate state and/or tort laws. If you work for a firm with *more* than fifteen employees, you must file with the EEOC before you can take your employer to court. Filing with the EEOC can be done without an attorney. (All EEOC forms can be obtained from your regional EEOC office; check the references in the back of this book.) The EEOC will decide if you can proceed with your charges. (Refer to page 125 for more details.) After the EEOC makes a decision, consult an attorney to evaluate your next move.

If you decide to proceed with legal remedies, have an experienced labor lawyer represent you. Don't try to represent yourself or hire an attorney without any experience with sexual harassment cases. Labor law is very complex and evolving, and choosing someone who does not have experience in this area can be exceedingly costly from both a time and monetary perspective.

A lawyer is an important and valuable resource. You can get the latest information about local, state, and national laws and legal tactics. In addition, an experienced attorney can provide insight and support; because our attorney had worked on so many of these cases, she was invaluable in reassuring us that the tactics that our respective companies were using were actually quite common.

Don't forget that an attorney (usually a team of attorneys) who has a lot of experience in employment and labor law will usually represent your company. Getting your own legal representation will protect you and level out the playing field a bit. And, as unfortunate as it is, you will most likely be taken more seriously if you have a lawyer represent you. Actually seeking help indicates to the company that you are serious about your claims, and that they should take them seriously, too.

The law regarding sexual harassment is so dynamic and complicated that, although we've attempted to explain some of the common legal strategies employed to defend against sexual harassment, every situation is unique, and without the benefit of an experienced professional, you may unnecessarily handicap yourself in your pursuit of a resolution.

Even though legal representation is strongly encouraged, *you do not have to get an attorney to file a private suit.* Filing a complaint in federal court without a lawyer is called a *pro se* complaint. Every district court has either a clerk or staff attorney who can assist you in filing *pro se.* To find out details on how to file a *pro se* complaint, contact the clerk of the court having jurisdiction over your case. He or she will be able to advise you of the appropriate person to contact and of the procedures to follow, which can vary from district to district.

Note: Whether you retain a private attorney or file *pro se,* you must file your suit in the appropriate court within ninety days of receiving your "right to sue" letter. See page 125 for more on EEOC filings and right to sue.

Because of the complicated nature of filing under Title VII of the Civil Rights Act and State Fair Employment Practices, you really should have a lawyer represent you. In addition, other compensatory and punitive remedies may be available under common tort law that an individual, without the aid of a lawyer, may not be aware of.

Note: Government employees have their own set of rules governing sexual harassment. These rules include special complaint procedures whereby the complaint process must be started within thirty days of the most recent incident of behavior. For information on sexual harassment policies and procedures for U.S. government employees, contact the EEOC.

Being Emotionally Prepared

Deciding to retain legal counsel can be one of the most excruciating decisions you'll have to make. This is not an easy windfall—rather, it is the beginning of a long, torturous process that will most likely only award you the satisfaction of knowing you did your part to end sexual harassment. Your employer will most likely lie about you, your co-workers may resent you for dragging them into the situation as witnesses, and the stress will take its toll on your personal relationships—not to mention on your physical and mental health.

Before doing anything, try taking a break to think things through. Only you can determine what outcome you'd like to see, and it's a good idea to know what that is before initiating action so that you are prepared should the company make a settlement offer.

If you feel overwhelmed by it all—and you will—talk to trusted friends and family or seek professional help. The feelings you will experience are not unique to you; they are a standard by-product of sexual harassment. You may wish to join a support group in which you can explore these feelings with other survivors of harassment. To locate a group near you, contact the National Organization for Women (NOW) and 9 to 5 chapters in your area. See page 177 and the Resource Guide for more information. As long as you do your homework and take a proactive approach in protecting yourself, you'll be OK.

Finding a Competent Attorney

When starting to search for a competent attorney, begin by speaking with friends, family, and trusted confidantes. Word of mouth is very important because a referral from someone who has been through a similar situation can give you a clear idea of what to expect and even prepare you for the consultation.

If this path turns up nothing, contact the local bar association, the EEOC, NOW, or one of the other organizations listed in the back of this book for a referral. Many can provide lists of attorneys in your area. You may also want to check out the Internet; many legal and state organizations can provide recommendations. There are also several attorney referral services operated by bar or other legal organizations.

Once you have several names, call the attorneys and ask about their experience with sexual harassment and discrimination cases.

The Consultation

Since lawyers are very busy people, most will interview you over the phone before even agreeing to set up a consultation. Regardless of who you are, your financial situation, or your position, they will ask you to recount salient facts about your case. They may even ask you to send them a copy of your log. If you pique their interest and your story rings true, then they will usually agree to meet with you. Don't be put off by all of the questions; this is simply a screening process to weed out false claims. With so much misinformation out there, reputable law firms are deluged with calls from people trying to turn misunderstandings and minor conflicts into serious cases of sexual harassment.

After a time is set up for the initial consultation, prepare yourself by reviewing your log and writing down any questions you would like to ask. Because the conversation is bound to become emotional, make a list of points you'd like to make before going in so that you don't forget to disclose everything you want to. You will be asked to tell your story in detail, and it is likely that the lawyer will have lots of questions for you. Some typical ones include:

- Do you have a log?
- Are there any witnesses?
- What was your reaction to each incident?
- Did you inform the harasser that the behavior was unwelcome?
- Did you follow the company's sexual harassment policy?
- Did you inform your supervisor?
- Who else at the company did you tell?
- What did they do and/or say?

There will also be questions about your employment history and the company itself:

- What is your salary history?
- How many employees are there in the company?
- Do you have or can you provide an organizational chart?
- How long have you been with the organization?
- How many positions have you held within the organization?
- Do you have and can you provide a copy of your company's sexual harassment complaint procedures?
- Do you have and can you provide a personnel manual?
- Do you have and can you provide your job description?
- Do you have and can you provide the initial job-offer letter?
- If you have resigned, do you have and can you provide a copy of your resignation letter?

In an effort to determine if there is any information that the company will use against you, you will be asked a series of very personal questions, possibly including:

- Is there anything that you know of that the company will use in its defense?
- Have you ever had a consensual affair with the accused?
- Have you ever had an affair with anyone else in the office?
- Have you ever received disciplinary or performance warnings? Have you ever been convicted of a crime?
- Have you ever attempted to file sexual harassment charges against a previous employer?

No matter how embarrassing the questions seem, it is important that you be honest and tell your lawyer everything so that he or she can best protect your interests. Remember that the organization has a lot at stake in your claim of sexual harassment and they will use everything they possibly can against you. The company's lawyers will do their best to portray you in the worst possible light, so if there is anything in your background that may be at all compromising, tell your lawyer so that he or she is not caught off guard by something that may be potentially embarrassing to you. Everything you tell your lawyer is bound by attorney/client confidentiality, so your lawyer cannot repeat anything you tell him or her.

Costs

Seeking legal representation is not an inexpensive venture. On average, a full-blown trial can run $75,000 to $100,000, plus an additional $4,000 to $25,000 for depositions, transcripts, and expert witnesses. Not to mention travel fees for the lawyer and miscellaneous hourly charges for photocopying, faxing, mail, and other clerical tasks. In major cities, the hourly fee for an experienced labor lawyer can be upward of $350.

The cost of the initial consultation is definitely worth the fee. As mentioned earlier, ask for a rate structure when you set up your initial appointment. If the lawyer agrees that you have a valid claim, the two of you can discuss whether you can afford the services outright or if other arrangements can be made. Many lawyers will evaluate your financial situation (don't be surprised if you are asked very personal financial questions) and the merits of your case. Be honest; this person is on your side. Even if the fee seems completely out of your price range, he or she may be able to suggest alternatives. In any event, it is advisable to get the fee structure in writing.

One popular option is contingency. Contingency usually means that the client is required to pay an up-front retainer and then a percentage of any settlement. Retainers (a "deposit" for your lawyer's services) can be almost any amount; it will be a point of negotiation between you and the lawyer. Typically the percentages required in a contingency situation run from 10 to 40 percent of any final judgment; this is usually negotiable as well. If you have faith that you have a good chance of a large jury award or settlement, consider asking to pay a larger retainer in exchange for a lower contingency percentage for the law firm.

Many law firms do not like to take cases on a "contingency only" basis; like most businesses, they like to know the victim has the ability to pay and a financial stake in the outcome. Taking a case on contingency usually tends to make a law firm pay a little more attention to avoiding unnecessary costs. It is a good sign if your lawyer wants to take your case on contingency structure as it indicates that he or she has faith in the strength of your case.

If You Can't Afford a Lawyer

If you do not have the resources to pay for a lawyer, most cities have legal aid societies and law clinics that may offer their services for a very small fee or even free (pro bono). They will offer references and help you find a low-cost attorney, usually one with an adjustable fee schedule.

Another option is to consult the U.S. district court that has jurisdiction in your area. They can assist you in finding a lawyer who will accept your case. You must file papers with the court requesting the appointment of counsel. Consult the office of the district court that assists *pro se* complaints for instructions on how to seek counsel. The appointment of counsel in any *pro se* complaint is always at the discretion of the court. They generally have a small filing fee (about $100) to begin a suit. However, if you truly can't afford it, the court may waive the filing fee. You are advised to ask the office of the district court that assists *pro se* complaints for information concerning the necessary procedure to request that the filing fee be waived.

If you seek outside legal counsel, you will have to pay the counsel unless it is taken on a contingency basis. Your company pays its own legal costs.

Filing with the Equal Employment Opportunity Commission

Have you filed a case with the EEOC? Have they investigated the situation? In most cases the EEOC will not investigate your claim. In the past the EEOC investigated all claims, but due to the exponential growth in caseload in recent years, and the agency's limited time and resources, it no longer can. It is still mandated that you wait 180 days after filing your EEOC claim for the EEOC to issue a "right to sue" letter. In many cases, a corporation may refuse to discuss an equitable settlement with the victim until after the victim has filed an EEOC claim and has waited the six months for the right-to-sue letter. A common strategy many companies employ is to make the 180-day window so unbearably uncomfortable that the victim quits her job and potentially forgoes a settlement and/or litigation.

Liability of the Employer

If, as a supervisor, you know about a harassment situation and take no remedial steps, the organization can be found legally liable. If the Human Resources Department does nothing, the courts will not tolerate the lack of action on their part and will likely find for the plaintiff. Under current law, employers do not become liable until they have (or until the point at which they should have) knowledge of the harassment and fail to act in a way "reasonably calculated to end the harassment." Courts will look at whether the employer had knowledge of the harassment and whether they made every possible effort to alleviate the situation.

Confidentiality and Mental Health Professionals

In June of 1996 the Supreme Court ruled that federal courts must allow psychotherapists and other mental health professionals the right to refuse to disclose patient records in judicial proceedings. By a vote of seven to two, the Court created a new evidentiary privilege, in both civil and criminal cases, similar to the lawyer/client and marital privileges the federal courts have recognized for years.

In the case of *Jaffee v. Redmond* (No. 95-266), Justice Stevens wrote that doctor/patient privilege would apply to clinical social workers as well as psychiatrists and psychologists because the reasons for having the privilege "apply with equal force" to all of these professions. He noted that clients of social workers often "include the poor and those of modest means." By making this judgment, Stevens made a great step toward protecting the rights of the poor in sexual harassment cases.

This decision brings the federal courts into line with the fifty states, all of which recognize some type of therapist/patient privilege. The Court's ruling is now part of Rule 501 of the Federal Rules of Evidence, and is now more inclusive than some of the state privileges.

What to Expect from the Company

Once the company was notified that I had hired a lawyer and was planning to file an EEOC complaint, they made my life even more miserable. Suddenly Human Resources personnel wanted to talk to me, my supervisor was being fed misinformation about what had happened, and although it was impossible to prove, I felt sure that management was treating me differently.

After the investigation was concluded and the results given to me via a memo, it became amazingly clear how far my co-workers would go to protect themselves. Although I should have known people would have no compunction about lying, it was my co-worker's lies that really stunned me. Despite all that happened, I believed that when push came to shove, people would tell the truth. It's incredible how morals and scruples can fly out the window when people's careers appear to be threatened. —Tracy

For me, my employer responded with intimidation and scare tactics. I was summoned while working and told I had ten minutes before I had to make a presentation. This presentation was made in front of the heads of legal counsel and Human Resources, and the managing director of the United States. At the time, I held my head up and felt that they were just testing my mettle. Now, in retrospect, I realize why they were probably doing it. They wanted to see what type of witness I'd make— whether I would be a credible witness. Would a potential jury believe me?

I came to believe that Human Resources was there to defend the company, regardless of the nature of the crime. It must be noted that it is not this way in every company. My former Human Resources Department acted from an old paradigm, in which they did not look on sexual harassment as a true problem for the organization, one that had deep roots and could affect overall morale. Instead my company decided to defend the most "valuable" employee. The most valuable was defined as the employee with a higher rank who made more money relative to the employee alleging the charges. As far as my company was concerned, they just wanted the "problem" to go away, and I was a constant reminder of the problem. They did not remove the serial harasser; instead they wanted me gone. In retrospect, they were probably concerned that the longer I remained with the organization, the higher the probability that I would talk to others about my situation.

In fact, I did stay with my former company until my 180 days were up and I received my right-to-sue letter. Many other employees, especially those who knew who I had worked with, came to me and told me stories about my harasser and how he had been guilty of the same offenses in other offices and was just moved around. I was told about other women who were experiencing the same sort of harassment by other people in the organization as well. These women—many of them chose to stay with the firm because they had worked too hard to get to a certain position, had children in school, or for various other reasons—had reported the situation according to prescribed channels, but their complaints, like mine, had fallen on deaf ears. I also heard the heartbreaking story of a former employee who had reported her situation of harassment to Personnel many times, with no resolution forthcoming, and feeling that nothing was changing, suffered a complete nervous breakdown. Hearing stories such as that made me more firm in my conviction that I had to continue my fight. If I didn't, they would win. Things would never change. I didn't have children in school to support. I didn't have to pay a large mortgage. If I didn't put my foot down, this horrible situation would continue. If I didn't step forward, who would?—Jane

When preparing for their defense, the company's legal representatives and Human Resources Department will try to obtain any information they can about you. In addition to the obvious things like performance appraisals, they will most likely recheck your references, review the résumé you gave them before you were hired, speak with your co-workers, and may even examine your phone records, computer files, and e-mail. Be sure to use care when speaking on the phone; refrain from making personal calls and don't speak about your case on your office phone. You should also refrain from sending personal correspondence via e-mail, and be aware that your computer files will most likely be read. During this time it is especially important to act in a highly professional manner. Don't do anything that you would not want made public.

Definitions of Common Legal Terms

During the course of your situation, you'll undoubtedly hear many legal terms bandied about. To aid in your understanding of the process, we've compiled a list of some common terms and their definitions.

Compensatory damages—Money awarded to individuals to make them whole or to place them in the position in which they would have been if the situation complained of had never occurred: actual losses.

Defamation—Oral (slander) or written (libel) false statement that damages another's reputation.

Defendant—Person or employer charged with the complaint or wrong.

Discovery—The learning of claims and damages and defenses of both sides. At this time, through the discovery process, employee, managers, and supervisors will be called upon to answer interrogatories (basically questions) and to testify under oath in depositions.

Hostile work environment—A type of sexual harassment marked by frequent, serious acts of a sexual nature that create the effect of a hostile, offensive, or intimidating working atmosphere. The victim need not show money damages.

Intentional infliction of emotional distress—Claim that the defendant intentionally acted in a way that he or they should have known would cause nontrivial emotional pain to another. The conduct must be so shocking or extreme that a person of normal sensibility would consider it an outrageous action.

Negligent hiring or retention—Tort action against employers who fail to protect employees from foreseeable harm by carefully checking references of new employees or failing to terminate employees who they know have caused harm in the past.

Plaintiff—The person bringing the lawsuit or EEOC claim, usually the victim in a sexual harassment case.

Punitive damages—Money awarded to an individual by the jury, or by specific statute, so that the defendant is punished for his conduct and so that all potential defendants will be effectively deterred from acting in the same manner.

Quid pro quo—Latin for "something for something." A type of sexual harassment marked by unwelcome activity of a sexual nature in exchange for tangible employment, or the loss of tangible job benefits because of the rejection of such activity.

Reasonable person/woman standard—The judicial standard of an individual who thinks and responds as an ordinary, logical, and careful person or woman would under the same circumstances and conditions.

Respondeat superior—Latin for "let the master answer." The principle that the master is responsible for the acts of the servant; usually meaning that an employer is responsible for the acts of an employee, whether or not the employer has actual knowledge of that employee's acts.

Sex discrimination—The favoring of one individual or group over another on the basis of gender or stereotypes associated with gender; recognized by Title VII and state statutes.

Sexist comments versus sexual harassment—Sexist comments include gender stereotyping, such as "It's a man's job to make money, a women's job to spend it" and "You're just a girl; what do you know?" Sexual harassment is a magnified version of sexism, consisting of specific sexist and sexual remarks directed at a particular individual. Often sexist comments are a precursor to harassment.

Sexual harassment—The imposition of unwelcome sexual conduct on a student or an employee in the workplace, which affects the student's or employee's performance.

Tort—A wrong committed by one person or institution against another, redressed by money damages.

Unemployment compensation—A claim for unemployment benefits does not bar other forms of legal relief. Unemployment benefits compensate those employees who lose their job through no fault of their own. Employees who quit their jobs may be able to collect such benefits upon showing sufficient cause for resigning.

CHAPTER 6
NAVIGATING THE LEGAL PROCESS

Courage is the price that life exacts for granting peace.
Amelia Earhart, *Courage,* 1927

If you've filed a complaint with your company and have not been able to resolve the situation appropriately, this chapter will help you navigate the legal process by explaining some of the basic claims and remedies that are available to you. Remember that while we have experience with sexual harassment and some legal remedies, we are not attorneys. This chapter is meant to provide an overview of what options are available to you. Since laws vary from state to state, you must check with Equal Employment Opportunity Commission (EEOC) and legal representatives from your own state. We have done our best to ensure that the information in this chapter is accurate, but in today's world of rapidly changing laws, it is best to seek professional help.

Informing the Company

Informing your employer of pending legal action is always nerve-shattering because you can never be sure of how management will react. Legally they cannot penalize you in any way for taking action to protect your rights, but in reality, they will do what they have to in order to protect themselves. If this means trying to get you to quit by making your life unbearable, they'll do it. If it means lying about you and portraying you in a negative manner, they'll do it. Often the ways that they penalize you are so subtle that it is difficult to prove unless you can show a pattern of behavior. That's why its so important to maintain your log even after you believe the situation has been resolved; you never know when you'll have to defend yourself.

Remember that it is illegal for an employer to fire you for filing an EEOC claim, seeking legal help, or suing to protect your rights. If the company does fire you—for any reason—seek legal assistance immediately. Obviously the company won't tell you that you've been fired because of your claims, so it's best to get outside assistance in proving your assertions.

The typical first step in the legal process is having your lawyer approach the company directly and ask for a settlement in exchange for a promise not to pursue further legal action. Many cases are settled at this point; once a victim has gone through the effort and expense to retain outside legal counsel, the company is often more likely to consider her claims. The flip side of this is that asking for a package puts the company on the defensive and they begin to rally their resources and may refuse to even consider your requests.

In other cases, the company may begin to consider your claims as valid and try to backpedal in order to protect themselves. This may mean that they will review their sexual harassment policy and try to take action, or they will start an investigation at this point.

It is almost a certainty that the company will immediately speak to their legal counsel the minute they receive notification from your lawyer. Don't be surprised if your boss sits you down and tries to glean information as to your future plans; the company is usually trying to determine how serious you are about pursuing this course of action.

State Agencies

Many states have agencies to resolve sexual harassment and employment discrimination issues. Usually these agencies function as mini EEOCs, but without the budget and time constraints faced by the larger agency. Contact your local EEOC office or local chapter of the National Organization for Women (NOW) for advice on locating a state agency.

Arbitration Committees

Many employers are now forming arbitration committees to resolve any employment discrimination issues, including sexual harassment. Often employers mandate that new hires sign an agreement stating that if any such issues arise, the employee will forfeit his or her rights to seek remedies through the legal system in favor of having the arbitration committee settle the dispute. While undoubtedly this solution is beneficial to the employer (no legal battles, no negative publicity, no costly judgments), the victim usually doesn't fare so well. Arbitration committees are aligned with the company in some manner— the members are either employees, are paid by the company to sit on this committee, or are somehow "friends" of the company. This immediately shades their neutrality.

If you sign such an agreement, you do lose all of your rights to seek other remedies. The Supreme Court has held up the validity of such documents (*Gilmer v. Interstate/Johnson Lane Corporation,* 500 US 20, 1991).

The EEOC and the "Right to Sue" Letter

The Equal Employment Opportunity Commission is a governmental body that was created to investigate and resolve issues of employment discrimination. Years ago, when sexual harassment and discrimination complaints were filed with the EEOC, each one was investigated by an EEOC staff member. Since the Anita Hill and Clarence Thomas hearings, the number of sexual harassment complaints has exploded exponentially and the EEOC simply doesn't have the manpower or budget to investigate every claim. Now filing with the EEOC is little more than a necessary formality; you must file with the EEOC in order to get "permission" to pursue a court case.

The EEOC has a deadline, or statute of limitations, for filing sexual harassment claims. *Typically you have 180 days from the last incident of sexual harassment to file a claim.* If you file with a state agency first, that deadline may be extended. Because laws vary from state to state and they are rapidly changing, call your local EEOC office for specific information on time frames and filing restrictions. It's also a good idea to find out if they will file a claim on your behalf with a state agency. (This may slow down the process.) Although this time window is available, it's best to file a claim right away. As with the caps on monetary damages (see page 132), the reasoning behind these deadlines is obscure, but make sure you adhere to them if you wish to file under the EEOC provisions.

In order to file a claim with the EEOC, there is a specific form that must be filled out. (We've included a sample of the form on page 200 so you would know what to expect.) The claim form in itself is not difficult to fill out; you simply need to provide a brief synopsis of what happened. A lawyer's advice is helpful here; he or she can help you to determine which facts are important and which can be left out.

Once the EEOC receives the form, they will send you a notification that they've gotten it and assign you a case representative. This representative is usually just a name to contact if you have questions; realistically he or she won't have the time to investigate your claim unless you file as part of a class-action suit, such as in the recent Mitsubishi case. The EEOC will notify your employer of complaints within ten days. When you file an EEOC charge, your name is divulged to your employer, but it will not be made public. If you file under a Fair Employment Practices Agency (FEPA) statute, then your employer will be served the complaint.

After 180 days you will receive a "right to sue" letter from the EEOC. Essentially this letter means that the EEOC will not bring a case on your behalf, but it does give you "permission" to file a claim. The letter will tell you whether the EEOC believes that sexual harassment occurred. Even if the EEOC does not state in the right-to-sue letter that they think harassment occurred, you may still sue. *However, you only have a window of ninety days to actually file a claim. After ninety days, your right to sue is relinquished.*

How the EEOC Processes a Claim

Although the EEOC does not have the staff to investigate every claim, they do look at some. Usually they will give you the option of waiting to have them review your claim, which can take months or even years, or receiving a right-to-sue letter as soon as the 180-day waiting period is finished. Most victims elect to take the right-to-sue letter so that they can move on with their lives—either by pursuing litigation or closing the case forever.

If the EEOC does review your claim, there are specific steps that are taken. Here is a brief overview of the process:

1. The complainant files an EEOC claim by filling out the form and stating the facts of the case.

2. Within ten days of receiving the complaint, the EEOC notifies the victim's employer that a claim has been filed. Usually a copy of the claim filed by the employee is forwarded to the employer.

3. The EEOC sends a lengthy questionnaire to the company in order to discover more information and give the employer the opportunity to explain their side. The information in this questionnaire may be "discoverable" if the case goes to court. In other words, the information may be released in the lawsuit.

4. The EEOC concludes the investigation. There are several possible outcomes:
   - If no reasonable or probable cause is found, the EEOC issues a Letter of Determination stating their findings. This does not mean that the victim cannot sue. She can request a right-to-sue letter and try to seek a favorable outcome in court. However, most attorneys would agree that if the EEOC finds no cause, it would be unwise to take further action.
   - If there is cause found, the EEOC may attempt to reconcile the case. If they cannot, they issue a right-to-sue letter, giving the victim ninety days to file a lawsuit.

- The EEOC files a lawsuit on your behalf. Although this is extremely rare, in especially egregious cases or in very large class-action suits (in which the plaintiff consists of a group of victims), they may decide to take action for you. One recent example of this is the Mitsubishi Motors case, in which a group of employees accused the auto manufacturer of creating an environment where sexual harassment was rampant.

To reiterate, the EEOC will probably never investigate your claim due to the growth in caseload and lack of funding. To enable victims to move on with their lives, the EEOC allows them to request the right-to-sue letter after 180 days—whether or not the claim was ever looked at. From the date that the letter is issued (not mailed or received), the victim has ninety days in which to file a lawsuit. After ninety days, the victim loses all rights to pursue a legal remedy for that particular claim.

When determining if a case has merit, the EEOC utilizes the following criteria:

Is the conduct unwelcome? The EEOC looks at the totality of circumstances; therefore it is important for the victim to clearly communicate that the conduct is unwelcome. This becomes particularly crucial in situations in which a prior consensual relationship may have existed. The EEOC will also try to determine whether the victim's conduct is consistent with the assertion that the sexual conduct was unwelcome.

The evidence of harassment. The resolution of a sexual harassment claim very often depends on the credibility of the parties. It is important that a victim's account be sufficiently detailed and internally consistent so as to be plausible. Lack of corroborative evidence where such evidence should logically exist undermines the allegation. By the same token, a denial by the alleged harasser will carry little weight when it is contradicted by evidence or a history of past behavior.

Is the work environment hostile? In order to violate Title VII, the harassment must be "sufficiently severe or pervasive" as to alter the condition of the victim's employment and create an abusive working environment. To determine hostile environment, the EEOC will look at:
- Whether the conduct was verbal, physical, or both
- How frequently it was repeated
- Whether the conduct was hostile or patently offensive
- Whether the alleged harasser was a co-worker or supervisor
- Whether others joined in perpetrating the harassment
- Whether the harassment was directed at more than one individual

In determining whether unwelcome sexual conduct rises to the "hostile environment" level in violation of Title VII, the EEOC will look at whether the conduct "unreasonably interferes with an individual's work performance" or creates "an intimidating, hostile, or offensive working environment." The reasonable-woman standard comes into play: would a "reasonable" woman be offended by the conduct? (For more on the reasonable-woman standard, see page 31.)

Negotiating a Settlement

Many times companies will attempt to negotiate a settlement in order to save the costs of a lengthy investigation, attorney fees, employee morale, and the company's image. Sexual harassment cases can turn into public relations nightmares. Companies may also attempt to settle with you to avoid the EEOC and state agencies investigating the business practices within the firm. It's a sad fact, but if a company has something to hide, such as shady business dealings or other discrimination or sexual harassment claims, then they will most likely settle.

Because a settlement offer can come at any time, know what you want before initiating any action. If your employer expresses an interest in negotiating a settlement, carefully consider the following issues:

Outplacement services: Outplacement services provide many benefits, including an office away from home, the camaraderie of others who were recently displaced, and advice and training on how to write your résumé, how to get through difficult interviews, and how to answer sensitive questions about why you left your previous job. outplacement services By may provide seminars, reference materials (such as journals and on-line databases), secretarial services, a phone, and a place to concentrate solely on the job search. Jane attributes much of her success in finding a new job so soon to the professional attention given to her career needs. By outplacement services many can provide a counselor who can help you with unresolved issues and, if he or she is a good match for you, really understands your situation. Jane was lucky to have an outplacement counselor who was finishing up law school with a concentration in labor law. She was reluctant at first to tell the counselor why she had left her job, but Jane soon realized that the counselor truly understood what she was going through. The counselor told Jane about other cases (generically of course) in which women she had worked with had experienced the same sexual harassment and had survived and had often found better positions. The counselor also helped repair

Jane's fragile self-esteem by pointing out all she had to offer a prospective employer.

Continuation of insurance: It comes as no surprise that insurance is expensive. Even if you do find a job immediately after leaving your company, sometimes new benefits packages do not start immediately. This is very important, as companies negotiate group benefits packages, and for what is usually a negligible amount of money, they can keep you on their insurance rolls for an additional six months (or whatever length of time you feel is necessary). If your family is covered by your insurance policy, it is even more important to attempt to include extended benefits coverage as part of your settlement package.

Good references: During a settlement, you can actually negotiate for good references. Often the company will agree to provide a letter of reference which you can forward to potential employers.

Money: You may feel that the only way to make you whole again is for the organization to pay monetary damages. Often at the beginning of settlement discussions the firm will offer you a small portion of your annual salary; in many cases they will offer you as little as a single month's salary. The amount of money that you are willing to accept is up to you, but it is wise to make sure that it will enable you to pay your bills while looking for another job.

New company policies: You may request that the company revise or institute a sexual harassment policy. Use your knowledge to educate others and to prevent others from being victimized. Chances are, they will be happy to listen to your advice because they will do everything to avoid a repeat of your situation.

What is negotiable is not limited to the preceding categories; this list is intended only to give you an idea of what is negotiable as part of the process. Don't be surprised if settlement talks take several rounds; as with any business negotiations, the company will start low and you will start high, only to meet somewhere in the middle.

The Settlement Document

After you and your employer agree on a settlement, you will be asked to sign a formal settlement document. If you don't sign it, your settlement package will not be given. Read it carefully; it may contain some provisions that you disagree with. Typically these documents have the following elements in common:

- The company won't admit guilt
- It will ask that you drop any current charges against the company
- It will ask that you not seek any further damages or relief against the company
- It will bind you to keep the details of the case and the settlement confidential

Damages as Allowed by the Civil Rights Act of 1991

There are caps as to how much money you can win in a court case. The Civil Rights Act allows for compensatory and punitive damages, but the amount of compensatory and punitive damages a victim can recover is limited to the size of the company:

$50,000 if the company employees 15–100 employees
$100,000 if there are 101–200 employees
$200,000 if there are 201–500 employees
$300,000 if there are 501 or more employees

This unfortunate cap on damages stops a lot of victims who have legitimate cases from filing with the EEOC. It boils down to a cost-benefit analysis: the realization that litigation could cost up to $100,000 and five years of their time, combined with the uncertainty of winning, causes many people to feel it is not worthwhile to pursue this. No state has a minimum number of employees greater than the fifteen described above. If you work for a company that employees fifteen or fewer employees, you must file a state or tort claim as you are precluded from filing with the EEOC to receive compensatory and punitive damages.

When the EEOC or an individual is pursuing a claim on behalf of more than one person, the damage caps are to be applied to *each aggrieved individual.* For example, if the EEOC files on behalf of ten complaining parties, against an employer who has six hundred employees, each complaining party may receive (to the extent appropriate) up to $300,000. The respondent's total liability for all ten complaining parties may be up to $3,000,000.

The law allows a complaining party to recover compensatory and punitive damages against a respondent who has engaged in unlawful intentional discrimination in violation of Title VII of the Civil Rights Act. *The damages available do not affect the right to back pay, front pay, or any type of relief already recoverable under Title VII.* Damages are authorized only in cases of intentional discrimination and are therefore not available when the charge alleges that neutral employment practices have an adverse impact.

As government employees are the only group excluded from the existing set of sexual harassment laws, and are covered by their own statutes, please refer to EEOC documents for the latest information. Victims who are union members should contact their union leader to obtain guidelines as to their specific grievance process.

Example of EEOC damages calculation: Sara is subjected to quid pro quo harassment and is subsequently demoted. As a result she suffers from severe depression. She spends $20,000 in psychiatric and medical bills for treatment of the depression. Her psychiatrist testifies that Sara will require two more years of therapy. She may also receive damages for the depression (nonpecuniary loss), damages for future psychiatric bills for the next two years (future pecuniary losses), and punitive damages. Her employer has ninety employees. The sum of the damages for the depression, future psychiatric expenses, and punitive damages cannot exceed the statutory cap of $50,000. Sara may receive $20,000 for the medical bills and full back-pay and front-pay awards, all of which are fully compensable and not included in the caps.

In states that allow money damages for personal injuries, the state law may provide your best avenue for pursuing your sexual harassment grievance. An example would be an employee in Florida who works for a firm that employs fewer than 150 people. This victim can prove damages of $850,000 for pain and suffering. Under Florida law, that person is entitled to the full amount. However, under the Civil Rights Act, because the company employs fewer than 150 people, the victim would only be entitled to $100,000. Even if your state does allow damages to compensate the worker for losses, it may not allow punitive damages to punish the harasser. The best legal defense (consult an attorney for specific information; do not rely on this text for legal guidance) might be a combination of both state and civil rights claims.

Here are brief descriptions of the types of damages that may be available to you:

Compensatory damages: This type of damages is awarded to compensate a victim for losses or suffering caused by the discriminatory act or conduct. They include damages for past pecuniary loss (out-of-pocket loss), future pecuniary loss, and nonpecuniary loss (emotional harm).

Pecuniary losses: Pecuniary means "of or relating to money." Pecuniary losses include moving costs; job-search expenses; medical, psychiatric, and physical therapy fees; and other out-of-pocket expenses that are incurred as a result of the sexual harassment. In order to recover damages, the victim must be able to prove that the harasser's conduct was the cause of the loss.

Future pecuniary losses: Future pecuniary losses are out-of-pocket expenses that are likely to occur after the resolution of the situation—for instance, future medical/psychiatric bills expected to be incurred. These are subject to the caps and do not include front pay.

Past pecuniary losses: These are not subject to the caps. The amount to be awarded for past pecuniary losses can be determined by receipts, records, bills, canceled checks, confirmation from other individuals, or other proof of actual losses and expenses. Damages for past pecuniary losses are not normally sought without supporting documentation.

Nonpecuniary losses: These are damages that are available to compensate the victim for "emotional harm." Emotional harm consists of a grouping of intangible injuries as emotional pain, suffering, inconvenience, mental anguish, and loss of enjoyment of life. Other nonpecuniary losses could include injury to professional standing, injury to character and reputation, injury to credit standing, loss of health, and other nonpecuniary losses that are incurred as a result of the discriminatory conduct.

Emotional harm may manifest itself as sleeplessness, anxiety, stress, depression, marital strain, humiliation, emotional distress, loss of self-esteem, excessive fatigue, or even a nervous breakdown. Physical manifestation of emotional harm may consist of ulcer, gastrointestinal disorders, hair loss, or headaches. An award for emotional harm is warranted only if there is sufficient causal connection between the respondent's illegal actions and the complaining party's injury. The discriminary act or conduct must be the cause of the emotional harm.

The claim of emotional harm will be undermined if the onset of symptoms of emotional harm preceded the discrimination. However, if a complaining party had preexisting emotional difficulties and his mental health deteriorates as a result of the discriminatory conduct, the additional harm may be attributed to the respondent. The fact that the complaining party may be unusually emotionally sensitive and incur greater emotional harm from the discriminatory conduct will not absolve the respondent from responsibility for the greater emotional harm.

Punitive damages: These are awarded to punish the defendant and to deter future discriminatory conduct. Punitive damages are available only when it can be proven that the respondent acted with "malice or with reckless indifference to the federally protected rights of an aggrieved individual." Punitive damages protect the victim from "future pecuniary losses, emotional pain, suffering, inconvenience, mental anguish, loss of enjoyment of life, and other nonpecuniary losses." They are not available against a federal, state, or local government, or government agency or political subdivision.

Calculation of Punitive Damage Amount

If malice or reckless disregard of the victim's rights is proven, the company may be liable for punitive damages up to the maximum amount allowed. The following factors are relevant in determining a defendant's financial position:

- Revenues and liabilities of the firm
- The fair market value of the company's assets
- The amount of liquid assets on hand, which includes amounts that they can reasonably borrow
- The respondent's ability to generate income in the future (projected earnings)
- The resale value of the business
- Whether the respondent is affiliated with, or is a subsidiary of, a larger entity that could provide additional financial resources

Other Alternatives

In addition to suing under Title VII of the Civil Rights Act, victims can seek damages under tort law as well as suing the harasser personally. These complicated legal maneuvers should be considered only on the advice of a competent attorney who specializes in employment law. Please refer to an attorney for specific information on tort law remedies for sexual harassment.

Legal Remedies for Harassed Employees

There are many legal remedies for victims. Some of the most common are as follows:

Constructive discharge as a result of harassment: To succeed in this claim, the employee may be required to leave his or her job within a reasonable amount of time after the last act of harassment or discrimination. The courts look to see if the company had a viable internal grievance procedure and how effective this procedure is in dealing with a hostile work environment.

Constructive discharge as a result of retaliation: A victim can use this claim if she can prove that she had an excellent work record until the time of her complaint but was fired based on a very sudden downturn of her work performance. In other words, if she was an exemplary employee, but as soon as she filed a claim, her employer suddenly claimed otherwise and she was fired, she can use constructive discharge as a basis for a legal claim.

Negligent hiring: This is based on the premise that an employer has a duty to protect its employees and customers from the risk of injury created by hiring an individual the employer knows, or should know, may harm others—for instance, if an employer knew that an employee had a history of sexual harassment but hired him anyway without regard to other employees within the firm.

Negligent supervision: The victim can claim that her employer negligently supervised the alleged harasser. In other words, the employer failed to take reasonable care in supervising a co-worker who posed a threat to others. An example would be Jane's situation. Her company knew that her harasser was a serial offender yet chose to retain him because he was a big income generator. They just reassigned him and his victims to other offices as necessary, never really dealing with the problem.

Negligent retention: When an employer discovers that an employee is unfit or dangerous, and if the employer fails to investigate or to reassign or terminate the employee, the employer may be held liable for negligent retention. This can be alleged in situations in which they move a known harasser from one office to another.

Intentional infliction of emotional distress: This is one of the most common charges in a sexual harassment claim and is one of the most litigated common-law theories of recovery. This charge is comprised of four elements:

1. Extreme and outrageous conduct
2. Intent to cause, or reckless disregard for the probability of causing, emotional distress
3. Severe emotional distress suffered by the complainant
4. The conduct complained of caused the complainant's severe emotional distress

There are also remedies that can be sought under breach of contractual claims. Speak to your lawyer to determine what course of action is best for your particular situation.

Employer Liability

Most plaintiffs take legal action against the employer because it is the company's responsibility to provide a professional working environment. If the company does not have a sexual harassment policy, or if it has one that is inadequate, then the company may be held liable for inadequate investigation and ineffective remedial action. In addition, a supervisor or co-worker who sexually harasses an employee can be ordered by the court to pay punitive damages out of his own pocket.

In some cases, managers are considered agents of the company and can be held personally liable. Although this is rare, check with your attorney to see if you have a valid claim against your supervisor or other member of your company's management.

An employer is responsible for its acts and those of its agents and supervisory employees with respect to sexual harassment—regardless of whether the specific acts complained of were unauthorized or even forbidden by the employer and regardless of whether the employer knew or should have known of their occurrence.

An employer will always be held responsible for quid pro quo cases because they are construed as the supervisor exercising the authority actually delegated to him. The supervisor's threatening actions are imputed to the employer whose delegation of authority empowered the supervisor to undertake them. The courts have held that because the supervisor was acting within the scope of his authority, this conduct may be fairly imputed to the employer. As such, the supervisor was using his authority to hire, fire, and promote to extort sexual consideration from an employee.

With hostile-work-environment claims, the employer is liable for the creation of a hostile environment by a supervisor when the employer knew or had reason to know of the sexual misconduct. An employer's knowledge of the situation can be evidenced by a complaint to management or an EEOC charge, the pervasiveness of the harassment, and evidence that the employer had deliberately ignored the problem by failing to establish a policy against it and a grievance mechanism to address it. Employers will also be thought to know of sexual harassment when it is openly practiced in the workplace or the situation is common knowledge among employees. This is often the case when there is more than one harasser or victim.

Hostile-environment claims are often coupled with claims of constructive discharge. The employer is liable for constructive discharge when it imposes intolerable working conditions in violation of Title VII. When those conditions compel a reasonable employee to quit, whether or not the employer specifically intended to force the victim's resignation, it is considered to be constructive discharge. The EEOC strongly encourages employers to "take all steps necessary to prevent sexual harassment from occurring, such as affirmatively raising the subject, expressing strong disapproval, developing appropriate sanctions, informing employees of their rights to raise and how to raise the issue of harassment under Title VII, and developing methods to sensitize all concerned."

CHAPTER 7

RETALIATION

The right way is not always the popular and easy way. Standing for right when it is unpopular is a true test of moral character.

Margaret Chase Smith, speech, Westbrook Junior College, Portland, ME, June 7, 1953

My claim was primarily one of retaliation. After the harasser was fired, I thought that I could continue to work for the man who, despite the harasser's own admission of his actions, had accused me of doing something to bring the behavior upon myself. This man had been reprimanded by the company because of my claims. I underestimated how angry he was. The tension between us was unbearable.

There were many signs of retaliation: I was the only person on my level to be denied business cards; I was not assigned a mentor; the accounting department actually asked why my time wasn't being billed to a clerical budget. Over time rumors got so bad that a memo was circulated saying that I had not been demoted. Of course, this just added fuel to the fire, and things got worse for me. Co-workers kept asking what I'd done to be demoted. It was absolutely humiliating to have to explain that I hadn't been demoted.

What is amazing is that after the investigation was concluded, they found no evidence of retaliation—everything could be explained away through a series of oversights. Despite *evidence to the contrary, they said that I had not been retaliated against. Yeah, sure.* —Tracy

After my company's investigation in which they found that I had been a victim of sexual harassment and presented me with a letter stating such, they offered me two choices: continue working in the same small regional office with the offender, or move to corporate headquarters to a similar position.

It was clear from the day I showed up at corporate headquarters that things had changed. I was told that I was being put on an "experimental project." I had no background in the designated area and no desire to be part of an experimental project. I couldn't understand what was happening. I had clearly been harassed and the corporation's investigation had ruled in my favor. I couldn't understand why I was now being punished. It was very clear that as a result of my reporting the harassment, the organization didn't want me to have any contact with "their" clients. I was no longer treated as part of the organization. I had become an outsider and was clearly treated as one. Even though the company said that they would not tolerate retaliation of any form, they treated me much differently than they did when I had been considered "one of them."

I resisted the offer of the "experimental project" job and repeatedly questioned Human Resources about the availability of other, more appropriate positions for my background and experience. They repeatedly told me that they didn't have anything suitable for me at the time, but they would look into finding me a permanent lending position. Meanwhile I was receiving news that other colleagues were being promoted into positions that would have fit my background nicely. To add insult to injury, instead of a private office as I had had in my previous location, I was only given a desk in the busiest part of the entire bank. Everyone entering the building or going anywhere else in the area had to pass by my desk to get there. Colleagues would constantly ask why I was on the "experimental project." The insinuation was that I really must have done something wrong to have been punished in this way. There were other simple yet telltale signs of retaliation, such as being denied business cards.

In my particular situation, when it became apparent that I was going to file an EEOC complaint, I resigned myself to attempt to make the best of the next 180 days (until it would be possible for me to proceed with legal remedies after receipt of my right-to-sue letter). I tried to make the situation as palatable and interesting as I could while I waited the 180 days. I attempted to control my resentment and do the work that was asked of me. As a result, I completed the project, and instead of just receiving a U.S. mandate for it, I also received a global mandate and an award for excellence from the head of the bank. It was very surreal, that I was being recognized for success in a certain endeavor while attempting to litigate with the firm for treating me unfairly.

Toward the end of my situation, I became more verbal. I was less embarrassed and more angered by what had happened to me in the regional office. When asked what precipitated the move back to New York, I started telling people that I had experienced "personnel difficulties." Other people started telling me similar stories of other women who had been harassed by my harasser. My corporation's solution to this problem was just to move the harasser to other offices (without, of course, warning the people in the new office).

In my situation, after the harassment investigation found in my favor, I was told that no retaliation would occur and I would be given the same type of position I had before the harassment began. My salary was not reduced, but I was put on a project I had absolutely no interest in. I had been in a marketing position and was all of a sudden assigned to an unrelated job.

As a result of completing the project, had my situation gone to trial, I believe I would have been on stronger legal footing than if I had just sat at my desk and refused to do the work that was assigned. They could have stated that I was incompetent, and that they felt this project was testing my competence, sense of being a team player, my devotion to the company, etc. In the end, the training in the new area actually permitted me to get a better job—I believe it allowed me to broaden my skills into a different area.—Jane

It is illegal for an employer to retaliate against someone who files a charge of discrimination, participates in an investigation, or opposes discriminatory practices. Employers are expressly prohibited from firing or discriminating against any employee or applicant for employment because he or she has made a complaint. If you believe that you have been retaliated against, contact the EEOC immediately. Even if you have already filed a charge of discrimination, you can file a new charge of retaliation.

The difficulty with retaliation claims is that they are extremely difficult to prove. Retaliation occurs after a sexual harassment claim is made, so the company is already aware that you are keeping track of everything that happens to you in order to build a case. In addition, it's common knowledge among the Human Resources Department and management team that retaliating against someone for filing such a claim is illegal. Therefore it's likely that all parties who are aware of the situation have been warned against taking any improper action against you.

However, this doesn't mean that retaliation won't occur; it simply means that it will be subtle and done in such a manner that it will be almost impossible to prove. In every case you are dealing with personalities, so when you make an accusation against someone, it's human nature for him to want to respond, whether that be through verbal confrontation or actions that are intended to "get even" with you. And when a company desperately wants to get rid of the problem, they will utilize subtle means to try and drive you out of the company. Because the company is torn between the desire for revenge or to be rid of you, and the knowledge that it is illegal, retaliation takes on almost imperceivable dimensions.

When dealing with retaliation, speak to trusted friends or family members about what is happening. It's easy for your judgment to become clouded; many people automatically assume that events that are taking place are a direct result of the claim. They could, in fact, be purely coincidental. Or you can be imagining that things are worse than they really are. Talking to someone objectively will help you to gain perspective on the situation as a whole.

What you should look for when trying to prove retaliation is a pattern. Isolated incidents may not seem to be much on the surface, but when you put several incidents together, then systematic retaliation becomes clearly evident.

How to Identify Signs of Retaliation

Retaliation is very subtle and can take on many forms. Although there are many more, here are some signs of retaliation that we encountered:

- Being transferred to a smaller area
- Being told there is not "adequate" or comparable position for you within the company
- Being moved to a position outside your scope of expertise
- Being demoted because of a reorganization
- Title and/or salary remains the same, but your job description changes for the worse
- Being denied business cards
- Being moved into a less desirable office
- Over time, your duties are slowly taken away from you

- You are moved to a project that underutilizes your abilities
- The company tries to "bore" you out of a job
- After a good work history, you are suddenly fired for poor performance
- You are degraded, treated poorly; intimidated or threatened
- You are introduced by a different title
- You are denied previous perks
- Your expense reports are audited
- You are treated differently than your peers
- There are allegations of incompetence or poor attitude
- You are accused of situations beyond your control
- Your projects are "sabotaged" by "faulty" equipment
- You are denied the resources necessary to do your job
- You are threatened with demotions or salary cuts
- Unfavorable information enters your personnel file
- You are laid off
- You are unfairly denied a promotion

When looking for retaliation, try to identify incidents that you honestly believe would not have happened had you not filed a sexual harassment claim. If you are one of forty people laid off during a reorganization, you will not be able to prove that it is retaliation. But if you are the only one laid off and the reason is a cutback, yet they keep less qualified, less senior employees, then it may be a retaliatory action.

Proving Retaliation

Due to the insidious nature of retaliation, it is very difficult to prove, even if the company does something as egregious as firing you. On an incident-by-incident basis, many forms of retaliation can easily be explained away as a legitimate action by the company. The best way to protect yourself is to take a proactive stance by building a case proving your value to the company and by documenting all possible incidents of retaliation:

- Keep a log. As with a sexual harassment claim, keep written records of every incident that could possibly be retaliation. Include items such as being denied resources necessary to do your job effectively, and evidence of other such incidents. See page 62 for more information on keeping a log.

- Keep copies of anything that serves as evidence of retaliation (e-mails, interoffice memos, etc). It's amazing what people will put in writing, and you will need to preserve any questionable documents. Print out any e-mails or memos right away; they have ways of getting erased.

- Gather evidence that people are being promoted to positions around you. For instance, if you have the exact qualifications for an internally posted position, yet you are told that the company will be looking outside the firm to select someone for the position because they do not have any employees who fit the profile, gather evidence to prove that you are qualified as well as all of the facts about the position itself.

- Keep copies of previous and current performance reviews. This could be important if, after you file a claim of sexual harassment, the company tries to fire you based on poor performance. Include information on salary history.

- Keep track of any awards you may have received, before, during, and after the sexual harassment. For instance, Jane won two performance awards while pursuing her sexual harassment claims. This would effectively nullify any claims of termination based on poor job performance.

- Keep a running log of what you are accomplishing on the job to ensure that you are appropriately recognized. Head off any claims that you are not performing up to par by keeping a detailed account of all of your projects.

- Keep track of any witnesses who may have seen signs of retaliation.

Immediately following your claim of harassment, try to head off any retaliation by watching your behavior and not doing anything that can even remotely be used against you. Do not take personal calls, talk on the phone excessively, or e-mail or fax anything that can be used against you. Make sure that your expenses reconcile to the penny. At this time, do all the work that is asked of you and more. Your may feel slighted at work and angry, but do your job to the best of your ability. Do not compromise your position by adapting negative work habits. If you feel the need to get even, do it legally.

Putting a Stop to Retaliation

As with a sexual harassment claim, you can bring attention to the fact that you are aware that you are being retaliated against and want it to stop by confronting the retaliators(s), filing a complaint with Human Resources, filing a complaint with the EEOC, and seeking legal advice. Consider retaliation as an off-shoot of sexual harassment, and take the same steps to protect yourself as you would in a harassment claim, such as keeping accurate records. If you have not sought legal help, you should do so now. Contact women's groups and other agencies for advice in hiring a lawyer.

When the retaliation is occurring, remember that you will not be in that situation forever. You need to focus on the next step, the step that will leave you in the best possible position once the horror of your ordeal is over and you move into the next phase of your life. This situation will not last forever; things will get better and you will survive. It's only a job, and you will find another one. And not every company will treat you in such a shoddy manner—there are companies out there that will truly value the skills you have to offer. The law is evolving in your favor, and the penalties for such harassing behavior are becoming so onerous that most firms are unwilling to tolerate sexual harassment and retaliation due to its impact, from both a financial and public relations perspective.

CHAPTER 8
PICKING UP THE PIECES OF YOUR CAREER

*To be brave in misfortune is to be worthy of manhood;
to be wise in misfortune is to conquer fate.*

Agnes Repplier, "Strayed Sympathies," Under Dispute,
1924

*For me, memories can be triggered by as little as a sound or a
glimpse of a certain scene. Although I left the company before
the issue was settled, even if the case had been resolved, I think
it would have been too emotionally painful for me to remain
in that environment. Certain areas—my own office included—
were inextricably linked to bad memories. Even today, a year
later, I feel a twinge when I hear the company's name mentioned.* —Tracy

*I sometimes feel like I have a post-traumatic stress disorder re-
lated to my harassment. Just when I think I've forgotten about
it, someone will mention the city where I experienced the harassment or I'll catch a glimpse of someone who resembles my
harasser on the street and I'll feel myself freeze like a deer
caught in headlights. I've gotten on with my life, I have a new
job that I enjoy, but I'm sometimes haunted by the memories of
an extremely painful time in my life.*

*Sometimes feelings that my rational side resists manage to
invade my thoughts: the irrational fear that maybe my career*

will be taken away again at a moment's notice, or some of the other feelings that my rational side knows are just ridiculous but that seem to paralyze me nonetheless, when I least expect them. It helped to talk through the feelings of loss with a trusted adviser as the separation almost felt like a death. I was made to quit my job, and did so without having another job to go to. I gave up quite a bit. So in addition to missing my work, my colleagues, and a sense of purpose, I had to pick up the shattered fragments of my self-esteem and look for another job.

Other fears resulted from the harassment:

- *I was frightened of my new employer finding out why I had left my previous job. It's difficult enough attempting to find a job without trying to explain a sexual harassment situation to a prospective employer.*
- *I knew I'd need references from my previous employer, but was unclear what they would say to a potential new employer.*
- *I knew I was not at fault, but still felt stigmatized by the fact that I had been a victim of sexual harassment.*
- *I knew I was a qualified professional who had a lot to offer a company, but felt marginalized by my harassment to the extent that I generalized the experience and felt that every future work environment would be the same.*
- *I lost faith in the system.*

—Jane

When going through our situations, both of us noticed that while the scant literature that was available on sexual harassment did touch on some important points, none of it addressed what happened after the harassment issue was resolved. As in that old public service announcement that shows a woman telling a harasser that she didn't have to take the abuse anymore, the available information was only helpful to a point. After the situation is resolved in the eyes of the law and the company, it is not over for the victim. This was just one of the reasons that we felt it was vital to share what we've learned. We've been there; we know that once the situation has been resolved to your satisfaction, life does not magically return to normal.

Even if you manage to settle with your company or win a big award from a jury trial, the pain does not disappear. There is a healing process that occurs—both emotionally and professionally. Typically victims spend so much time, energy, and emotion dealing with the abuse that when it is resolved, there is almost a "crashing" feeling. Suddenly this all-consuming effort is gone and there is a gaping void. It's like emerging from a long, dark tunnel and being blinded by dazzling sunlight; for a few moments you are completely immobilized.

Taking a few days to get used to life again is therapeutic. But then reality sets in and you are expected to continue on with things as if nothing ever took place. This is when you must pull together the pieces of your career and refocus your energies on your job. And this is often easier said than done.

In most cases you are likely to find yourself looking for employment elsewhere. If the company offered you a settlement package or you pursued litigation, then chances are, you and the company have agreed upon a "mutual separation." This means that although you didn't quit and the company didn't fire you, the two parties agreed that it would be best to sever the relationship. And depending upon your package, you should have some time in which to find a new job.

However, once the situation has reached a conclusion—you file with the EEOC but decide against litigation; the company transfers either you or the harasser to another location; or the harasser is fired—you now have the choice of resuming your career with the same organization or moving on to a new position elsewhere. As with every other decision you've had to make during this process, this is a highly personal one. Only you can determine whether you can handle remaining in the same environment.

Staying with the Company After the Situation is Resolved

Some people have the ability to immediately put an unpleasant ordeal behind them. Others carry the memories in the forefront of the mind for a long time to come. It's easy to lapse into memories. Simple things like a scent or a sound can suddenly bring a flood of emotion. That's why you need to carefully consider whether the job is worth remaining in the same environment that was once so laden with fear, anger, and abuse that it was physically difficult to go there every day. Only you can determine which type you are and whether you can handle staying with the same company after the harassment has ended.

Spend a few days reacclimating to the environment without the issue of harassment hanging over you. View things as objectively as possible. See how your co-workers and manager treat you. Then sit down and take inventory of your feelings. If you feel even the slightest bit uncomfortable in your surroundings, you need to seriously consider seeking other employment. Eventually these feelings may interfere with your ability to do your job. For some people it is helpful to keep a journal of their thoughts and feelings in dealing with something as traumatic as returning to the place that caused so much pain and grief.

If you are considering remaining with the company, ask yourself the following questions:

- Do you believe that the company will not hold the situation against you during performance reviews and when it comes time for promotions?
- Can you salvage relationships with co-workers who were hostile during the investigation?
- Will you be treated as an equal?
- Have your relationships with vendors and/or clients remained unscathed?
- Do you have enough confidence in yourself to handle any negativity?
- Has your harasser been fired or transferred?
- Will your co-workers remain neutral about the situation? Will they refrain from being hostile?

If you answer no to any of these questions, you need to think very carefully about the pros and cons of leaving. You don't have to pick up and quit right away; you can continue to work there while actively searching for employment elsewhere. In fact, it may be a good idea to remain. As many career counselors advise, it is easier to find a job when you are already employed.

In Tracy's case, the harasser was fired and she assumed that her working environment would return to normal. However, she was retaliated against. Her immediate supervisor held a grudge because he had been reprimanded by the company, co-workers kept asking questions as to why the harasser was suddenly gone, and those involved in the situation began to do some politicking to restore their reputations. All of this added up to a very uncomfortable situation for Tracy; although she never wanted to think of the harassment again, it provided fodder for the gossips to latch on to. It was literally months before things died down, and even then the situation didn't return to normal. No matter what happened or how much time had passed, there was still a stigma attached.

If the harasser is transferred, there are still all of the questions as to why he suddenly disappeared. And depending upon the structure of the organization, you may come into contact with him in the future. If you feel there is absolutely no chance of contact, or if you can handle being in touch with him, then this is not so much of an issue. But if you tense up when you hear his name, or are fearful of the mere possibility of contact, then seriously consider changing jobs.

Another issue to deal with is the attitude of your co-workers. Depending upon the climate during the sexual harassment situation, your co-workers may blame you for stirring up trouble, getting the harasser into trouble, or changing the atmosphere of the workplace. Or, as in Jane's case, your co-workers may be so thoroughly disgusted by the way you were treated that they applaud you for taking a stand. In Tracy's case, while publicly her co-workers spewed the company line, privately they would come up to her and praise her for her actions. They couldn't voice their true feelings publicly because they were afraid that the company would turn on them. Even though co-workers were publicly aligned with the organization, they offered to help Tracy find legal representation. Because the fear of retaliation is so pervasive, don't be surprised if people say one thing privately yet do another thing publicly.

The situation is a bit easier if you are the one transferred. Assuming that the transfer is a positive move for you careerwise, then you have the chance to work in an entirely new environment, with new faces, and with no reminders of the harassment.

If you do decide to remain with the company after the harassment issue has been resolved (even if you are transferred), take a close look at your career goals and realistically examine your future opportunities with the organization. While they will tell you that there will be no retaliation at all, you must look at the signs they are giving and decide for yourself if you can have a bright future at the company. Consider also the psychological ramifications of remaining in the same physical environment. You may wish to discuss the situation with trusted friends, family members, or a health care professional.

Starting a New Career Somewhere Else

Many women decide to remain in the same job because of financial constraints or a perceived difficulty in finding comparable employment. However, you never know what you will find until you look. It won't hurt to send out résumés while continuing at the company. Seek the advice of an outplacement service; speak with a career counselor. You needn't tell them the details of your situation; you can position the move as a step toward a new career goal or state that you are simply exploring new opportunities. The important thing to realize is that you are never trapped; from this point onward, the only limitations and restrictions on your life are ones you put on yourself.

Handing in Your Resignation

When putting together a resignation letter, you may want to consult legal counsel to make sure that you do not compromise your legal standing with the company. From a semantic perspective, you need the language in your resignation letter to allow you to retain your legal rights. Tracy's attorney wrote her resignation letter, stating exactly why she was leaving— because the sexual harassment situation had created a hostile and unhealthy working environment. Ironically, the company sent a responding letter denying any evidence of a "hostile environment."

Don't neglect to hand in a written resignation; you don't want to give the company the opportunity to claim that you abandoned your position.

To Tell or Not to Tell

I told my current boss about what had happened at my previous company. It was she who suggested informing Human Resources and, in turn, telling the president and CEO. After careful consideration, I followed her advice.

My primary motivation for doing this was that the corporate headquarters for my previous employer was in the same area as my new office, and I knew for a fact that the CEO of the new company was involved in a project with an executive from the old one. This book was also planned, and I figured that he'd certainly find out about my harassment experience once it was published. Rather than take the chance that somehow he would find out, I decided to tell him myself.

It was frightening. As I walked down the corridor to his office, I relived all of the horrible memories of telling my story to the investigators and management team of the other company. And I really didn't know this person. I suspected that he would be fair and wouldn't hold the situation against me—but I didn't know for sure how he'd react.

He heard my story and asked some questions, but he was very fair and didn't make any judgments about my professional abilities based on what I told him. In fact, when I told him about our plan to write the book, he was very supportive.

I am very lucky to be working for a company that is so progressive and takes a firm stance against all forms of discrimination. I'm also lucky to be working in a younger, more forgiving industry than Jane.

Looking back, I am happy with my decision to inform the company I now work for because I don't have to worry about them finding out by other means. —Tracy

I have decided not to inform my new employer about what had happened to me. When they asked me why I left the previous firm, I honestly told them that my previous project had been completed successfully and the learning curve had flattened— I was ready for a new challenge.

As much as I believe in full disclosure, I didn't want to plant a seed of doubt in the eyes of my new supervisors—I didn't want them to think that I was somehow incompetent, asked for, or solicited the behavior in any way. I did not want the stigma of sexual harassment to follow me to my next job. I was ashamed that I had been involved in the situation in the first place, and I didn't want to bring it with me into the next phase of my life.

Admittedly, the fact that I work in a very conservative old-boy industry had some bearing on my decision to remain quiet about the harassment.

I was concerned about the small size of the industry, but those who knew of my past were happy to see me at a new organization and were disgusted when they saw how unfairly I had been treated by my former employer. —Jane

As with all of the decisions you will be faced with during your ordeal, the question of whether to make your situation known to your new employer is an extremely personal one. What was right for Tracy was not right for Jane; neither may be right for you. Here are some points to keep in mind when thinking about it:

It's a small world. Many industries can be likened to sparrows sitting on a telephone wire: There is always the same number of spots to sit, and there is always the same number of sparrows. The only difference is that after they get up and fly around, they switch spots. In other words, your new co-worker may be someone from your old company, or your new boss may run into your old one at a seminar. Consider the likelihood of your old world colliding with your new one and how the story of your ordeal can be leaked to your new company. Is it better in the long run for you to tell the company or for them to find out on their own? Does it matter to you? Or is it highly unlikely that they could ever find out?

Image is important. In some industries, especially traditionally conservative ones such as banking or finance, or male-dominated ones such as medicine or industrial products, being known as a victim of harassment can be detrimental to your career. In some circles, even the mere mention of sexual harassment is scandalous. Even if someone's hiding a "dirty little secret," it's more important to look pulled together and professional than it is to do what is right and solve the problem.

There is a stigma attached. As unfair as it is, sexual harassment brands you. In some people's minds it can make you seem "hysterical" and "emotional" for taking action and not simply accepting the abuse. To others, you may seem "loose" or "cheap" for "causing" the sexual harassment to happen.

Because people's perception is their reality, whatever they think to be true will be true in their minds. And since a person's perception is based upon his or her very personal view of the world, you can never predict what someone's reaction will be. For this reason, you may find it best to simply keep the situation to yourself and avoid any possible negativity.

Not all companies are in the dark ages. There are thousands of companies to work for out there, and not all are run by men who believe that sexual harassment doesn't exist. Only you can gauge how progressive the company is with its sexual harassment and antidiscrimination policies.

You want to put the incident behind you. For some women, the only way to heal and to move on with their lives is to "compartmentalize" the harassment and keep it confined to one part of their lives. Carrying it forward to a new job would only serve to keep the incident alive.

Other women feel strongly that it is a part of them, and that they have learned and grown from it. By telling their story, they are encouraging their own healing process by helping stamp out harassment and keeping others from being victimized.

You are ashamed. Although there is absolutely no reason to be embarrassed or ashamed by what you went through, it is perfectly normal to have these feelings. What you know logically is often diametrically opposed to what you feel in your heart. Just remember, what happened to you is not your fault.

You refuse to be ashamed. Being victimized by sexual harassment is nothing to be embarrassed about. You shouldn't have to keep part of your life under wraps—if you don't want to. However, you needn't prove the point by telling everyone who walks by. Spreading the word as to what happened won't dull the edge of pain associated with it.

Although it's unlikely that any company would be so unthinking as to knowingly take action against an employee because she was victimized by sexual harassment while working elsewhere, their impression of the victim could be shaded. Whenever they think of this person, it could be in conjunction with the words *sexual harassment.*

Certain factors become indelibly linked to a person, and an incident such as sexual harassment is one of them. As with most decisions you will have to make during your ordeal, this one is highly personal and only you can weigh the particular factors involved and make a decision that you can live with.

CHAPTER 9
THE HEALING PROCESS

Time heals all wounds.
Proverb

Unless you have firsthand experience with sexual harassment, you cannot imagine how it can consume your entire life and make you question your fundamental sense of self. In a short period of time you undergo a metamorphosis from a savvy professional to an insecure shadow of your former self. Once the abuse and its aftermath have abated, it takes time and a lot of work to rebuild your self-esteem. Life does not return to the way it was before the harassment—the ordeal is one that you will carry with you for a long time. Hopefully, though, you can learn from it and emerge stronger than before.

Sexual Harassment as a Severe Stressor

To get a sense of how traumatic this type of incident can be, consider the American Psychiatric Association, which recognized sexual harassment as a potential "severe stressor" in the

Diagnostic and Statistical Manual of Mental Disorders, 11 (3d Ed. 1987) ("DSM-111-R"). Sexual harassment is not the type of situation that one can leave at the office; it comes home with you and permeates every aspect of your life. It takes a toll on personal relationships; many men cannot handle seeing their partner crumple under the stress. It is also not something that you can just walk away from and forget; the damage it does to the very core of your self-esteem, the self-doubt that it creates, the fear and anger, become a part of your personality. After living in such an environment, it becomes impossible to shed the side effects.

It is not possible to measure the exact stress of sexual harassment in your life, but with the help of the Stress Scale, developed by University of Washington medical school researchers Thomas H. Holmes and Richard H. Rahe in 1965, it is easier to put it in perspective. This scale was designed to rate an individual's risk for illness in general and is widely regarded as a useful predictor of depression. Listed below are the "events" and their "value," with 100 being the highest:

Death of spouse	100
Divorce	73
Marital separation	65
Jail term	63
Death of close family member	63
Personal injury or illness	53
Marriage	50
*Fired from work	47
Marital reconciliation	45
Retirement	45
Change in family member's health	44
Pregnancy	40
Sex difficulties	39
Addition to family	39
*Business readjustment	39

*Change in financial status	38
Death of a close friend	37
*Change to different line of work	36
Change in number of marital arguments	36
Mortgage or loan over $10,000	31
Foreclosure of mortgage or loan	30
*Change in work responsibilities	29
Son or daughter leaving home	29
Trouble with in-laws	29
Outstanding personal achievement	28
Spouse begins or stops work	26
Starting or finishing school	26
Change in living conditions	25
Revision of personal habits	24
*Trouble with boss	23
*Change in work hours, conditions	20
Change in residence	20
Change in schools	20
Change in recreational habits	19
Change in church activities	19
Change in social activities	18
Mortgage of loan under $10,000	17

Source: "The Social Readjustment Rating Scale," reprinted from the Journal of Psychosomatic Research, Volume II, T. H. Holmes and R. H. Rahe, 1967, Pergamon Imprint, Oxford, England.

Note that the asterisks* indicate incidents that are often a part of, and a direct result of, sexual harassment on the job; and they are not mutually exclusive. Sexual harassment is insidious in that it affects your work life and your relationships at the same time. When sexual harassment is coupled with retaliation, one may have to quit one's job, have one's self-esteem destroyed, and have relationships collapse, all as the situation at work is reaching a crescendo. This domino effect can happen at a time when you lose your job, have a legal battle on your hands, and undergo financial difficulties. This terrible intersection of important events can deliver a crushing blow to your relationships all at the same time due to sexual harassment on the job.

Studies reveal that:
- 25 percent of women use sick leave or personal time in order to avoid harassing situations
- Of those who experience harassment, 10 percent leave their place of employment
- 50 percent attempt to ignore it
- Women who ignore sexual harassment undergo a 10 percent drop in productivity
- Women who recognize that they are being sexually harassed experience a 2 percent drop in productivity

Source: Klein Assoc., Inc., Working Woman *Sexual Harassment Survey (1988).*

The five-stage grieving process as described by Elisabeth Kübler-Ross is a good way to look at the stages of dealing with sexual harassment on the job because, in effect, you are mourning for life as it used to be: the professional aspects and the personal aspects. It's important to recognize that these stages are not linear: they can overlap or you can move back and forth through them. The final stage of acceptance of what has happened to you and recognition that you are normal will help in your recovery process. Seeing a psychiatrist or mental health professional to talk through things that are bothering you will also help to speed your recovery process.

In detail, the five stages of grieving are as follows:

1. Denial

Example: "I can't believe that the company conducted an investigation and they ruled in my favor, yet they no longer want me at the firm." "They wouldn't treat me like this, I've been a loyal employee all these years."

Honesty is a good way to deal with this stage. Realize that the organization may not be "fair"; many firms choose to side with the "most valuable" employee (the one who makes the most money for the firm or provides the most benefits to the organization). Emotional nurturing is important at this stage to help the individual rebuild her self-esteem. Participate in support groups in which you can speak with others who are experiencing the same type of ordeal; it will help to provide perspective and to balance how you view the situation. Realize that it is not your fault that you are being victimized; place the blame where it belongs—on the harasser. Tell yourself that this is just a curve that life has thrown you; cling to the belief that everything will turn out all right. This type of attitude will help you on the road to recovery.

2. Bargaining

Example: "Maybe if I go to Human Resources and ask for my job back again, they will listen." "Maybe if I convince them that I was wronged, they will treat me justly."

In this stage you must do something for yourself in order to survive. Be proactive; focus your energies on healthy activities. You can send out résumés, start working out at the gym, take classes in night school, start networking, or whatever feels right for you. At this point most people acknowledge that they probably will not be able to stay with their employer and realize that they will be better job candidates if they learn a new skill, hone an existing one, etc. You must work on yourself and start positioning yourself for recovery. It will improve your self-esteem and allow you to feel more in control.

3. Anger

Example: "Why is this happening to me?" "I try to be a good person and stay out of trouble, so why am I living this painful experience?"

At this stage you get mad and may even start to doubt some of your own basic beliefs. The anger may be directed at anyone and everyone: men in general, the corporation, people who try to help, your attorney, your friends and family, or even at yourself for falling prey to sexual harassment. This anger can easily become displaced and can hurt the people you love the most, such as family and friends. In a marital or close relationship, you need the correct foundation to weather a difficult storm such as this. At this point it is important to vent feelings of anger in a safe environment such as to a social worker, support group, a psychologist or psychiatrist, or a close and trusted friend. The listener should be nonjudgmental and supportive and allow you to voice your feelings of anger. Even if you are irrational, it is helpful to voice this anger and get rid of it before it resurfaces in other areas of your life.

4. Depression

Example: "My life is never going to get any better." "I'll never be able to be happy again."

This is probably the most difficult stage to deal with; it is often the point at which people finally realize that they have been victimized by sexual harassment. Suddenly there is an overwhelming feeling of sadness and emptiness. Suddenly the activities that provided a sense of happiness are no longer pleasurable. It's common to become withdrawn or nervous, and to have powerful feelings of worthlessness and guilt. It is also common to experience insomnia, lack of concentration, and a sluggishness and lethargy that no amount of rest can overcome. Recurrent thoughts of suicide are also common when one is experiencing the effects of depression.

The fear of the unknown, such as having to find a new job and possibly litigate, often leads to depression. So does the feeling of being alone in dealing with sexual harassment. There is also a sense of powerlessness accompanied by the harassment—the knowledge that although you saw the debacle gathering steam, you were unable to do anything to stop it. The feeling of a loss of control, which is so common for a victim of sexual harassment, also serves to make a bad situation even worse.

At this stage what you have to do is attempt to turn the lemons into lemonade. You need anchoring, and to feel a sense of purpose outside of yourself. Achieve this by becoming a volunteer, exercising, practicing yoga, meditating, spending time at church, talking to other people who are experiencing the same thing as yourself. Eat well, work on hobbies, take classes you've wanted to take, rest, and do nice things for yourself. Force yourself to rejoin life.

Note: Seek professional help if your sense of depression begins to become all-consuming. If you have any thoughts of suicide, seek professional help immediately.

5. Acceptance

Example: "Yes I was victimized by sexual harassment, but I won't let it break me." "It wasn't fair, but things will be a OK."

At this stage you need to focus on what you are going to learn from the ordeal. Realize that as bad as things are right now, it's not going to last forever, and maybe you can use what happened to help others through education, support groups, and dissemination of information.

Look at the past in an objective fashion and explore ways of using what you've learned. As the old saying goes, "What doesn't kill you makes you stronger." Use this strength and knowledge in other aspects of your life. Use the situation to learn more about yourself.

Markers of Depression

Depression is a syndrome. To diagnose it, most physicians use the criteria listed in the *Diagnostic and Statistical Manual of Mental Disorders* (DSM-IV) of the American Psychiatric Association. The criteria are:

- Depressed mood most of the day
- Marked diminished interest or pleasure in activities
- Significant weight loss or gain when not dieting (more than 5 percent of body weight a month), or decrease or increase in appetite nearly every day
- Insomnia or hyperinsomnia almost every day
- Psychomotor agitation or psychomotor retardation—an abnormal speeding up or slowing down of one's activities and mental processes
- Fatigue or loss of energy nearly every day

- Feelings of worthlessness or excessive or inappropriate guilt
- Diminished ability to think or concentrate, or indecisiveness, nearly every day
- Recurrent thoughts of death (not just fear of dying) or suicide without a specific suicide attempt or specific plan for committing suicide

To qualify as a major depressive disorder, in addition to the first or second symptom, at least five of the others must be present during the same two-week period.

If you are experiencing these symptoms or believe that you may be suffering from a depressive disorder, seek professional help immediately.

Feeling Better

I have never admitted this to anyone but my doctors, but what truly led me to seek help were my overwhelming thoughts of suicide. I was trying so hard to handle my sexual harassment by myself. I was working harder, smarter, winning awards for my performance on the job, yet the harassment was not going away. I thought maybe if I stayed out of the office, it would go away, but it didn't.

I remember walking home from work with a colleague and he described to me how someone in his apartment complex had committed suicide the night before. Instead of feeling horrified, I felt envious that this person didn't have to deal with the hell I called life. I found myself just wanting to sleep all day, yet when I got home at night, I couldn't sleep. I kept ruminating about the ordeal and how I could possibly make it end. I really wish that I had sought help earlier, as I could have possibly avoided some of the deleterious long-term effects of the depression. —Jane

There is a very big difference between what you know to be true intellectually and what you feel to be true emotionally. Sexual harassment is a difficult thing to deal with; suddenly you are questioning what you know to be true and experiencing irrational feelings.

Even though I know this wasn't my fault, I still felt that maybe somehow I could have done something to avoid it. And although I'm embarrassed to admit it, sometimes I think back and wonder if I could have altered the course of the situation. Yes, I know that I was victimized by someone else's abusive behavior, but I still experience lingering feelings of guilt and shame. —Tracy

To keep yourself strong, you must focus on doing something healthy for yourself. You may feel as if you are being pulled in many different directions, and friends and family may be telling you to "get over it," "don't make a mountain out of a molehill," "it's only a job," and "deal with it," but you must find time to experience your feelings and to work through them. Here are some ways that we kept sane during the experience:

Exercise: Exercise is good for both your physical and psychological well-being. As difficult as things were for us, exercise was a real release. When approaching the breaking point, an aerobics class or a good run was enough to provide the energy needed to continue the fight. Exercise helps to raise the spirits and lifts mild depression. It provides much-needed energy and a sense of accomplishment. Exercise is a great way to deal with the stress of sexual harassment, although it is better as part of a larger program of therapeutic solutions such as family, friends, counseling, support groups, and religion.

Family: It is important that you tell your family what is happening in the workplace. Even if you pride yourself on solving your own problems, you can't handle this issue by yourself. Be open with your family and friends about what is happening. Many people involved in sexual harassment are too close to the situation to remain objective; and in losing your objectivity, you may suffer much more than you would if you confided in your family and friends.

It wasn't until I was seriously contemplating suicide that I knew things had gotten out of control. I was obviously not handling things as well as I thought I was. I knew I needed help and I knew I needed it immediately. I shudder to think what may have happened if I didn't go to the phone book and call a psychiatrist, after one particularly insidious incident with my harasser. I really felt that I wanted to end the pain of what I was going through. I didn't realize that it wasn't my fault at the time. All I knew was that I kept working harder, longer, and smarter, and instead of the pain going away, it just got worse. There were days when I absolutely dreaded going to work and actually manifested physical illness when I thought I would have to see my harasser. If I had told my family earlier, they would have provided the support and objectivity that I so obviously and desperately needed. They would have made it clear (as they did later) that it was my harasser who had the problem and not me. I had internalized things for far too long. I highly recommend that you seek the help of trusted family members as soon as possible to minimize the potential harm.
—Jane

Friends: Many people don't want to bother friends with the gory details of sexual harassment. However, not telling your friends only serves to reinforce your sense of isolation. There is no benefit to proving that you are tough by keeping the situation to yourself; true friends will sense that there is something going on. Good friends are there for you in difficult times, and in such a stressful time of your life, the coping skills that you use for other difficult situations are generally not applicable and usually don't work. Although its very difficult to speak to trusted colleagues about what is happening, sometimes doing so can help you realize that you are not alone. In Jane's case, had she opened up to her colleagues earlier, she would have found out that the same man victimized others as well.

Individual counseling: To avoid the inherent bias of dealing with friends and family, a trained psychiatric professional can provide an objective evaluation of what you're going through. In addition, he or she may have encountered a similar situation with other patients and may leave you with the feeling that your reaction to such a severe psychiatric stressor is normal and expected, given the gravity of what you were dealing with on a daily basis.

Support groups: As the prevalence of sexual harassment grows, more support groups to deal with it will be formed. It is a good idea to join one to vocalize your feelings about your ordeal. There are many similarities in sexual harassment behavior, and you will learn effective coping behaviors from others that have dealt with the same thing. Support groups are often led by a trained psychiatrist or social worker, who will help with an unbiased interpretation of the situation and your reaction to it. Just knowing that other people have experienced that same sort of abuse and survived is wonderfully comforting. Learning how others picked up the pieces of their lives can help you tailor your own specific coping strategy. This is a proactive way to deal with the harassment and discover ways of avoiding it in the future.

Women's organizations: Groups like the National Organization for Women and 9 to 5 exist to help people like us. Use them as a resource; by being able to speak to someone who understands what you've gone through, you remove the sense of isolation. They can offer legal advice and support groups, and can help you to prepare for your next step in the battle. They are a tremendous resource and should be tapped.

Religion: A trusted clergy member is a valuable source of comfort with a situation as difficult as sexual harassment on the job. In addition, utilizing your own personal worship methods to examine appropriate ways to handle it can also prove effective.

Will I Ever Be the Same Again?

Although its very tempting to say yes, you will be the same, the real answer is no. You've been through a terribly traumatic incident, and you will carry those memories around forever. The issue is how you will deal with what you've been through: will you learn and grow from it, using your knowledge and experience to help others, or will you carry the hurt and anger around forever?

You will be whole again. You will learn to trust again. You will be happy again. But you will never forget what happened. Take this experience and use it to benefit yourself. Become involved in helping your company create a comprehensive sexual harassment policy; volunteer to speak about your experience at a support group; help someone else experiencing the situation to locate resources, or just be a sympathetic ear in a time of need. Do your best to help prevent sexual harassment from happening to others.

RESOURCE GUIDE

National Organizations

Women's Legal Defense Fund
1875 Connecticut Ave. NW,
    Ste. 710
Washington, DC 20009
202-986-2600

National Women's Law Center
1616 P Street NW, Ste. 100
Washington, DC 20036
202-328-5160

National Organization for
    Women
1000 16th Street NW, Ste. 700
Washington, DC 20036
202-331-0066

National Council for Research
    on Women
47-49 East 65th Street
New York, NY 10021
212-724-0730

NAACP Legal Defense and
    Education Fund
99 Hudson Street
New York, NY 10013
212-219-1900

Mexican American Legal De-
    fense and Education Fund
1430 K Street NW
Washington, DC 20005
202-628-4074

Federation of Organizations for
    Professional Women
2001 S Street NW, Ste. 500
Washington, DC 20009
202-328-1415

Equal Rights Advocates
1663 Mission Street, Ste. 550
San Francisco, CA 94103
415-621-0672 (office)/415-621-
    0505 (info)

Coalition of Labor Union
  Women
15 Union Square
New York, NY 10003
212-242-0700

Center for Women Policy
  Studies
2000 P Street NW, Ste. 508
Washington, DC 20036
202-872-1770

Business and Professional
  Women's Foundation
2012 Massachusetts Ave. NW
Washington, DC 20036
202-293-1200

American Arbitration Assoc.
  Center for Mediation
1660 Lincoln Street, Ste. 2150
Denver, CO 80264-2101
303-831-0823/800-678-0823

Association of American Col-
  leges Project on the Status
  and Education of Women
1818 R. Street NW
Washington, DC 20009
202-387-3760

Asian-American Legal Defense
  and Education Fund
99 Hudson Street
New York, NY 10013
212-966-5932

American Federation of
  Teachers, Women's Rights
  Committee
555 New Jersey Ave. NW
Washington, DC 20001
202-879-4400

Women Employed
22 Monroe, Ste. 1400
Chicago, IL 60603
312-782-3902 (job problem hot
  line)

NOW Legal Defense and Education Fund
99 Hudson
New York, NY 10013

9 to 5: National Association of
  Working Women
614 Superior Ave.
Cleveland, OH 44113
216-566-9308

National Women's Law Center
11 Dupont Circle NW, Ste. 800
Washington, DC 20036
202-588-5180

National Employment Lawyers
  Association (NELA)
535 Pacific Ave.
San Francisco, CA 94134
415-227-4655

Fund for the Feminist Majority
1600 Wilson Blvd., Ste. 704
Arlington, VA 22209
703-522-2501 (hot line)

Federally Employed Women
1400 I Street NW, Ste. 425
Washington, DC 20005
202-898-0994

Equal Rights Advocates
1663 Mission Street, Ste. 550
San Francisco, CA 94103
415-621-0505 (hot line)

Equal Employment Opportu-
    nity Commission (EEOC)
800-669-4000 (help line)
813-893-1141 (office)
813-344-5555 (hot line)
    Florida (counseling)

Alabama

Equal Employment Opportu-
    nity Commission
1900 3rd Avenue North, Ste. 101
Birmingham, AL 35203-2397
205-731-0082

Alaska

Alaska State Commission for
    Human Rights
800 A Street, Ste. 202
Anchorage, AK 907-276-7474

Alaska Women's Resource
    Center
111 West 9th Street
Anchorage, AK 99501
907-276-0528

Arizona

Attorney General's Office, Civil
    Rights Div.
1275 West Washington Street
Phoenix, AZ 85007
602-542-5263

EEOC
4520 North Central Ave., Ste.
    300
Phoenix, AZ 85012
602-640-5000

Arkansas

Equal Employment Opportu-
    nity Commission
425 W. Capitol, Ste. 625
Little Rock, AR 72201
501-324-5060

California

California Department of Fair
    Employment and Housing
2014 T Street, Ste. 210
Sacramento, CA 95814
916-227-2878/800-884-1684

Univ. of California, Santa Cruz
Title IX/SH officer
109 Clark Kerr Hall
Santa Cruz, CA 95064
408-459-2462

University of California, San
  Francisco
Women's Resource Center
San Francisco, CA
415-476-5836

Univ. of California, Davis/The
  SH Educ. Prog.
Guilbert House, 112 A Street
David, CA 95616
916-752-9255 (office)/916-752-
  2255 (hot line)

Defense de Mujeres
406 Main Street, Room 326
Watsonville, CA 95076
408-722-4532 (office)/408-685-
  3737 (hot line)

Golden Gate University Law
  School/Women's Empl.
  Rights Clinic
536 Mission Street
San Francisco, CA 94105-2968
415-442-6647

Equal Rights Advocates
1663 Mission Street
San Francisco, CA 94103
415-621-0505 (help line)

University of California at San
  Francisco
Women's Resource Center
415-476-5836

EEOC
96 North Third Street
San Jose, CA 95113
408-291-7352

EEOC
901 Market Street, Ste. 500
San Francisco, CA 994103
415-744-6500

EEOC
401 B. Street, Ste. 1550
San Diego, CA 92101
619-557-7235

EEOC
1333 Broadway, Room 430
Oakland, CA 94612
510-273-7588

EEOC
3660 Wilshire Blvd., 5th floor
Los Angeles, CA 90010
213-251-7278

EEOC
1313 P. Street, Ste. 103
Fresno, CA 93721
209-487-5793

Parents for Title IX
P.O. Box 835
Petaluma, CA 94953
707-765-6298 (SH in schools)

Colorado

Colorado Civil Rights Commission
1560 Broadway, Ste. 1050
Denver, CO 80202
303-894-2997

Discrimination and Sexual Ha-
rassment Support Group
(DASH)
Boulder Nat. Org. for Women
P.O. Box 7972
Boulder, CO 80306
303-444-7217

EEOC
1845 Sherman Street, 2nd floor
Denver, CO 80203
303-866-1300

Connecticut

Connecticut Women's Education and Legal Fund
135 Broad Street
Hartford, CT 06105
203-865-0188 (office)/203-524-
0601 (info)

Connecticut Commission on
Human Rights and Opportu-
nities
90 Washington Street
Hartford, CT 06106
203-566-3350

Connecticut Commission on
Human Rights and Opportu-
nities
1229 Albany Avenue
Hartford, CT 06112
203-566-7710

Connecticut Women's Education and Legal Fund
135 Broad Street
Hartford, CT 06105
203-247-6090

Delaware

Delaware Department of Labor,
Antidiscrimination Section
4425 N. Market Street
Wilmington, DE 19809
302-761-8200

Delaware Department of Labor
State Office Building/ 820
North French Street, 6th floor
Wilmington, DE 19801
302-577-2882

Contact Delaware
P.O. Box 9525
Wilmington, DE 19809
302-761-9800 (crisis)/800-262-
9800 (in-state)

District of Columbia

Federally Employed Women
1400 Eye Street NW
Washington, DC 20005
202-898-0994

D.C. Commission on Human
   Rights
2000 14th Street NW, 3rd floor
Washington, DC 20009
202-939-8740

D.C. Office of Human Rights
441 4th Street NW, Ste. 970 N.
Washington, DC 20001
202-724-1385

Georgetown Sex Discrimination Clinic
202-662-9640

EEOC
1400 L Street NW, 2nd floor
Washington, DC 20005
202-275-7377

U.S. Department of Labor,
   Women's Bureau
200 Constitution Ave. NW
Washington, DC 20210
800-827-5335

Wider Opportunities for
   Women
815 15th Street NW, Ste. 916
Washington, DC
202-683-3143

Florida

Florida Commission of Human
   Relations
325 John Knox Road, Bldg. 5,
   Ste. 240
Tallahassee, FL 32303-4149
800-342-8170/904-488-7082

Human Relations Department,
   City Hall
400 South Orange Ave.
Orlando, FL 32801-3317
407-246-2122

Family Service Center
2960 Roosevelt Blvd.
Clearwater, FL 34620
813-530-7233

EEOC
501 East Polk Street, 10th floor
Tampa, FL 33602
813-228-2310

EEOC
1 Northeast First Street, 6th floor
Miami, FL 33132
305-536-4491

Lawyer Referral Service
407-422-4537 (lawyer referrals)

Georgia

Georgia Commission on Equal
  Opportunity
156 Trinity Avenue SW, Ste. 208
Atlanta, GA 30303-3654
404-656-1736

9 to 5: National Association of
  Working Women
250 10th Street NE, Ste. 107
Atlanta, GA 30309
404-616-4861/800-669-0769

Georgia Commission on Equal
  Opportunity
710 Cain Tower
Peachtree Center/229
  Peachtree Street NE
Atlanta, GA 30303
404-656-7708

EEOC
10 Whitaker Street, Ste. B
Savannah, GA 31401
912-944-4234

EEOC
75 Piedmont Ave. NE, Ste. 1100
Atlanta, GA 30335
404-331-6093

Hawaii

University of Hawaii at Manoa,
  Office of Sexual Harassment
  Counselor
2600 Campus Road, Room 210
Honolulu, HI 96822
808-956-9499

Hawaii Civil Rights Commission, Enforcement Division
888 Mililani Street, 2nd floor
Honolulu, HI 96813
808-586-8636 (admin.)/808-
  586-8640 (complaint)

EEOC
677 Ala Moana Blvd., Ste. 404
Honolulu, HI 96813
808-541-3120

Idaho

Idaho Human Rights Commission
450 West State Street, 1st floor
Boise, ID 83720
208-334-2873

Idaho Commission on Human
  Rights
P.O. Box 83720
Boise, ID 83720-0040
208-334-2873

Idaho Woman's Network
P.O. Box 1385
Boise, ID 83701
208-344-5738

Illinois

Illinois Department of Human Rights/James R.Thompson Center
100 West Randolph Street, Ste. 100, 10th floor
Chicago, IL 60601
312-814-6245

YWCA—Women's Services
180 North Wabash
Chicago, IL 60601
312-372-6600

Women Employed
22 West Monroe, Ste. 1400
Chicago, IL 60603
312-782-3902

EEOC
536 South Clark Street, Room 930A
Chicago, IL 60605
312-353-2713

Indiana

Indiana Civil Rights Commission
100 North Senate Ave., Room N103
Indianapolis, IN 46204
317-232-2600/800-628-2909

Indiana Civil Rights Commission
Indiana Government Center N103
Indianapolis, IN 46204
317-232-2600/800-628-2909

Information and Referral Network/General Referral Service
3901 North Meridien
Indianapolis, IN 46208
317-926-4357

EEOC
46 East Ohio Street, Room 456
Indianapolis, IN 46204
317-226-7212

Iowa

Iowa Civil Rights Commission
211 E. Maple Street, 2nd floor
Des Moines, IA 50319
515-281-4121

Women's Resource and Action Center
University of Iowa
317-335-1486

Kansas

Kansas Commission on Human
  Rights
Landon State Office Bldg.
900 SW Jackson, Ste. 851S, 8th
  floor
Topeka, KS 66612
913-296-3206

Kentucky

Kentucky Commission on Human Rights
332 W. Broadway, Ste. 700
Louisville, KY 40202
502-595-4024/800-292-5566

EEOC
600 Martin Luther King, Jr.,
  Place, Ste. 268
Louisville, KY 40202
502-582-6082

Louisville–Jefferson County
  Human Relations Commis-
  sion
200 South 7th Street
Louisville, KY 40202
502-574-3631

Lexington-Fayette Urban
  County Human Rights Commission
162 East Main Street, Ste. 226
Lexington, KY 40507
606-252-0071

Louisiana

Equal Employment Opportu-
  nity Commission
701 Loyola Ave., Ste. 600
New Orleans, LA 70113-9936
504-589-2329

EEOC
701 Loyola Ave., Ste. 600
New Orleans, LA 70113
504-589-2329

Maine

Maine Human Rights Commission
State House, Station No. 51
Augusta, ME 04333
207-624-6050

Maine Women's Lobby
P.O. Box 15
Hallowell, ME 04347
207-622-0851

Maryland

Maryland Commission on
  Human Relations
6 St. Paul Street, Ste. 900,
  9th floor
Baltimore, MD 21202
410-767-8600/800-637-6347

EEOC
111 Market Place, Ste. 4000
Baltimore, MD 21202
301-962-3932

Maryland Commission on
  Human Relations
20 East Franklin Street
Baltimore, MD 21202
410-767-8600

Massachusetts

Massachusetts Commission
  Against Discrimination
McCormack State Office Bldg.
1 Ashburton Place, Room 601
Boston, MA 02108
617-727-3990

Cambridge Women's Center
46 Pleasant Street
Cambridge, MA 02139
617-354-8807

Women's Crisis Center
24 Pleasant Street
Newburyport, MA 01950
508-465-2155

Massachusetts Commission
  Against Discrimination
1 Ashburton Place, Room 601
Boston, MA 02108
617-727-3990 (Boston)/413-
  739-2145 (Springfield)

EEOC
1 Congress Street, Room 100,
  10th floor
Boston, MA 02114
617-565-3200

Michigan

Michigan Department of Civil
  Rights
1200 Sixth Ave., 5th floor
Detroit, MI 48226
313-256-2663

WINGS
P.O. Box 4793
Troy, MI 48099
810-437-8091

EEOC
477 Michigan Ave., Room 1540
Detroit, MI 48226
312-226-7636

Michigan Department of Civil
  Rights
333 South Capitol
Lansing, MI 48913
517-373-3590 (Lansing)/313-
  876-5544 (Detroit)
517-373-2884 (women's commission)

Minnesota

Minnesota Department of Human Rights
500 Bremer Tower
Seventh Place & Minnesota
Street
St. Paul, MN 55101
612-296-5663/800-657-3704

Minnesota Women's Consor-
tium
5555 Rice Street
St. Paul, MN 55103
612-228-0338

Chrysalis
550 Rice Street
St. Paul, MN 55103
612-222-2823 (office) 612-871-
2603 (resource line)

Mississippi

EEOC, Jackson Area Office
207 W. Amite Street
Jackson, MS 39201
601-965-4537

Gulf Coast Women's Center
P.O. Box 333
Biloxi, MS 39533
601-435-1968

Missouri

Missouri Commission on
Human Rights
3315 W. Truman Blvd./P.O. Box
1129
Jefferson City, MO 65102
314-751-3325

EEOC
625 North Euclid Street,
5th floor
St. Louis, MO 63108
314-425-6585

EEOC
911 Walnut, 10th floor
Kansas City, MO 64106
816-462-5337

YWCA Women's Resource
Center
140 North Brentwood Ave.
Clayton, MO 63105
314-726-6665

Women's Self Help Center
2838 Olive Street
St. Louis, MO 63103
314-531-9100 (office)/314-531-
2003 (hot line)

Montana

Montana Human Rights Division/Department of Labor and Industry
616 Helena Ave.
Helena, MT 59620
406-444-2884/800-542-0807

Nebraska

University of Nebraska Women's Center
117 Nebraska Union
Lincoln, NE 68588-9446
402-472-2597

Nebraska Human Rights Commission
State Office Bldg., 301 Centennial South, 5th floor
Lincoln, NE 68509
402-471-2024

Nevada

Nevada Equal Rights Commission
1515 East Tropicana, Ste. 590
Las Vegas, NV 89119
702-486-7161

Crisis Call Center
P.O. Box 8016
Reno, NV 89507
702-323-4533

New Hampshire

New Hampshire Commission for Human Rights
163 Loudon Road
Concord, NH 03301
603-271-2767

Womankind Counseling Center
21 Green Street
Concord, NH 03301
603-225-2985

University of New Hampshire Sexual Harassment and Rape Prevention Center (SHARP)
Huddleston Hall
Durham, NH 03824
603-862-3494 (8:00 A.M.–4:30 P.M.)/603-862-1212 (after 4:30)

New Jersey

Women's Referral Central
800-322-8092

EEOC
60 Park Place, Room 301
Newark, NJ 07102
973-645-6383

YWCA
140 East Hanover Street
Trenton, NJ 08608
609-989-9592 (office)/609-989-9332 (hot line)

Rutger's Law School Women's
  Rights Litigation Clinic
15 Washington Street
Newark, NJ 07102
973-648-5637

New Jersey Division on Civil
  Rights
383 West State Street
Trenton, NJ 08618
609-292-4605

New Jersey Division on Civil
  Rights
303 West State Street, CN090
Trenton, NJ 08625
609-292-4605

New Mexico

New Mexico Human Rights
  Commission
1596 Pacheco
Santa Fe, NM 87502
505-827-6838

EEOC
505 Marquette NW, Ste. 900
Albuquerque, NM 87102
505-766-2061

New York

New York State Division of Hu-
  man Rights
Alfred E. Smith State Office
  Bldg./P.O. Box 7063
Albany, NY 12225
518-474-2705

NOW NYC Help line
105 East 22nd Street
New York, NY 10011
212-260-4422

EEOC
90 Church Street, Room 1501
New York, NY 10007
212-264-7161

EEOC
208 Church Street, Room 301
Buffalo, NY 14202
716-846-4441

9 to 5: National Organization of
  Working Women
63 Jerusalem Ave.
Hempstead, NY 11550
516-485-6787

Jefferson County Women's
  Center
120 Arcade Street
Watertown, NY 13601
315-782-1855

New York State Division of Human Rights/Office of Sexual Harassment Issues
55 Hanson Place, Ste. 346
Brooklyn, NY 11217
718-722-2060/800-427-2773

North Carolina

North Carolina Human Rights Commission
117 West Jones Street
Raleigh, NC 27603-1334
919-733-7996

North Carolina Equity
505 Oberlin Road, Ste. 100
Raleigh, NC 27605
919-833-4055 (business)/800-451-8065 (hot line)

EEOC
1309 Annapolis Drive
Raleigh, NC 27601
919-856-4064

EEOC
801 Summit
Greensboro, NC 27405
336-333-5174

EEOC
5500 Central Ave.
Charlotte, NC 28212
704-567-7100

North Carolina State Office of Administration Hearings
424 North Blount Street
Raleigh, NC 27601
919-733-2691

North Carolina Human Relations Commission (private employees)
121 West Jones Street
Raleigh, NC 27603
919-733-7996/800-699-4000

North Carolina Council for Women
James K. Polk Bldg.
500 West Trade Bldg./P.O. Box 360
Charlotte, NC 28202
704-342-6367 (Charlotte)/
910-334-5094 (Greensboro)/
704-251-6169 (Asheville)/
919-514-4869 (New Bern)/
919-83-6595 (Greenville)

North Dakota

North Dakota Department of Labor
State Capitol, 600 E. Blvd., 6th floor
Bismarck, ND 58505
701-328-2660/800-528-8032

University of North Dakota
   Women's Center
305 Hamline Street
Grand Forks, ND 58203
701-777-4300

Ohio

EEOC
1375 Euclid Ave., Room 600
Cleveland, OH 44115
216-522-2001

EEOC
525 Vine Street, Ste. 810
Cincinnati, OH 45202
312-353-2713

Victims Advocacy Program, The
   Link
315 Thurston Ave.
Bowling Green, OH 43402
419-352-5387 (office)/800-472-
   9411 (hot line)

9 to 5: National Organization of
   Working Women
615 Superior Ave. NW
Cleveland, OH 44113
216-566-9308 (office)/216-621-
   9449

Ohio Civil Rights Commission
Southeast Regional Office
220 Parsons Ave.
Columbus, OH 43266
614-466-5928

Women's Policy Research Commission
30 E. Broad Street, Ste. 2701
Columbus, OH 43266
614-466-5580/800-282-3040
   (hot line)

Committee Against Sexual Harassment (CASH)
YWCA
65 South 4th Street
Columbus, OH 43215
614-224-9121

Ohio Civil Rights Commission
220 Parsons Ave.
Columbis, OH 43215
216-379-3100 (Akron)/
   513-/852-3344 (Cincinnati)/
   216-787-3150 (Cleveland)/
   614-466-5928 (Columbus)/
   513-285-6500 (Dayton)/
   416-245-2900 (Toledo)

Oklahoma

EEOC
531 Couch Drive
Oklahoma City, OK 94612
405-231-4911

Oklahoma Human Rights Commission
2101 North Lincoln Blvd.,
   Room 480
Oklahoma City, OK 73105
405-521-2360

Resonance Listening and
    Growth Center for Women
1609 South Elwood Avenue
Tulsa, OK 74119
918-587-3888

Oregon

Oregon Bureau of Labor and In-
    dustries/Civil Rights Division
State Office Bldg.
800 N.E. Oregon
Portland, OR 97201
503-731-4075

Pennsylvania

EEOC
1000 Liberty Ave., Room 2038 A
Pittsburgh, PA 15222
412-644-3444

EEOC
1421 Cherry Street, 10th floor
Philadelphia, PA 19102
215-656-7020

Women's Law Project
125 South Ninth Street, Ste. 300
Philadelphia, PA 19107
215-928-9801

Women's Alliance for Job Equity
    (WAJE)
1422 Chestnut Street, Ste. 1100
Philadelphia, PA 19102
215-561-1973

Philadelphia Commission on
    Human Relations
34 South 11th Street, 6th floor
Philadelphia, PA 19107-3654
215-686-4692

Pennsylvania Human Relations
    Commission
711 State Office Bldg.
Broad and Spring Garden
Philadelphia, PA 19130
215-560-2496

Pennsylvania Human Relations
    Commission
101 South Second Street,
    Ste. 300
Harrisburg, PA 17105-3145
717-787-9784 (Harrisburg)/412-
    565-5395 (Pittsburgh)

Rhode Island

Brown University
Sara Doyle's Women's Center
401-863-2189

Rhode Island Commission for
    Human Rights
10 Abbott Park Place
Providence, RI 02903
401-277-2661

South Carolina

EEOC
15 South Main Street, Ste. 530
Greenville, SC 29601
803-241-4400

Crisisline
803-271-8888

South Carolina Human Affairs
    Commission
2611 Forest Drive/P.O. Box 4490
Columbia, SC 29240
803-253-6339/800-521-0725

South Carolina Human Affairs
    Commission
2611 Forest Drive
Columbia, SC 29204
803-253-6336/800-521-0725

Center for Women
20 Mary Street/P.O. Box 22095
Charleston, SC 29413
803-722-4909

South Dakota

South Dakota Division on Hu-
    man Rights
State Capitol Bldg./222 East
    Capitol, Ste. 11
Pierre, SD 57501
605-773-4493

Tennessee

Tennessee Human Rights Com-
    mission
Capitol Blvd. Bldg.
530 Church Street, Ste. 400
Nashville, TN 37243
615-741-5825

EEOC
50 Vantage Way, Ste. 202
Nashville, TN 37228
615-736-5820

EEOC
1407 Union Ave., Ste. 621
Memphis, TN 38104
901-722-2617

Tennessee Human Rights Com-
    mission
530 Church Street, Ste. 400
Nashville, TN 37243
615-741-5825

Texas

EEOC
5410 Fredericksburg Road,
    Ste. 200
San Antonio, TX 78229
210-281-7600

EEOC
1919 Smith Street, 7th floor
Houston, TX 77002
713-653-3377

EEOC
The Commons, Bldg. C, Ste. 100
El Paso, TX 79902
915-534-6550

EEOC
8303 Elmbrook Drive
Dallas, TX 75247
214-767-7015

University YWCA Women's
  Counseling and Resource
  Center
55 North IH35, Ste. 230
Austin, TX 78702
512-472-3053

Texas Civil Rights Project
512-474-5073

The Dallas Rainbow Now Sexual Harassment Support
  Group
608 Whistler
Arllington, TX
817-792-3736

Texan Commission on Human
  Rights
8100 Cameron Road, Bldg. B,
  Ste. 525
P.O. Box 13493
Austin, TX 78753
512-837-8534

Women's Advocacy Project
P.O. Box 833
Austin, TX 78767
512-476-5377

Utah

Utah Women's lobby
P.O. Box 1586
Salt Lake City, UT 84114
801-530-6801

Utah Industrial Commission, Antidiscrimination Division
160 East 300 South
Salt Lake City, UT 84110
801-530-6801

Vermont

Vermont Attorney General's Office Division
109 State Street
Montpelier, VT 05609
802-828-3657

Vermont Human Rights Com-
  mission
135 State Street/Drawer 33
Montpelier, VT 05633-6301
802-828-2480

Virginia

EEOC
3600 West Broad Street, Room
  239
Richmond, VA 23230
804-278-4651

EEOC
252 Monticello Ave./SMA Bldg.,
　　1st floor
Norfolk, VA 23510
804-441-3470

Council on Human Rights
1100 Bank Street, Washington
　　Bldg., 12th floor
Richmond, VA 23219
804-225-2292

Fairfax Human Rights Commission
12000 Government Center
　　Pkwy, Ste. 318
Fairfax, VA 22035
703-324-3953

Alexandria Human Rights Commission
110 N. Royal, Room 201
Alexandria, VA 22035
703-324-2953

Washington

EEOC
2815 Second Ave., Ste. 500
Seattle, WAS 98121
206-553-0968

Washington State Human Rights
　　Commission
711 S. Capital Way, Ste. 402/P.O.
　　Box 42490
Olympia, WA 98504-249
206-753-6670/800-233-3247

Northwest Women's Law
　　Center
119 South Main Street, Ste. 330
Seattle, WA 98104
206-621-7691

West Virginia

West Virginia Human Rights
　　Commission
1321 Plaza East, Room 106
Charleston, WV 25301
304-558-2616

Center for Economic Options
601 Delaware Avenue
Charleston, WV 25302
304-345-1298

Wisconsin

EEOC
310 West Wisconsin Ave., Ste.
　　800
Milwaukee, WI 53203
414-297-1111

Wisconsin Department of In-
　　dustry, Labor and Human Re-
　　lations/Human Rights
　　Division
201 East Washington Ave.,
　　Room 402
Madison, WI 53708
608-266-6860

9 to 5: National Association of
    Working Women
238 W. Wisconsin Ave., Ste. 700
Milwaukee, WI 53203
414-274-0925

Women's Center Collective
P.O. Box 581
Sheridan, WY 82801
307-672-7471/307-672-3222
    (hot line)

Wyoming

Wyoming Fair Employment
    Commission
US West Bldg./6101 Yellow-
    stone Road, Room 259C
Cheyenne, WY 82002
307-777-7261

APPENDIX
SAMPLE DOCUMENTS

The following documents are included to give you an idea of the paperwork that you will receive from the United States Equal Employment Opportunity Commission (EEOC). Please be aware that these are only samples; the EEOC updates their forms regularly, and you should contact them if you want to file a claim.

The documents are as follows:

> Document 1: General information on filing a suit, provided by the EEOC.
>
> Document 2: Form to be filled out by charging party when submitting a claim to the EEOC.
>
> Document 3: Form to be filled out by claimant and her attorney after determining the charge of sexual harassment.
>
> Document 4: Form letter sent out by the EEOC to acknowlege receipt of a claim.
>
> Document 5: Form letter sent to charging party and employer to acknowledge that charges have been

withdrawn (either because a settlement has been reached or because the claim has been withdrawn).

Document 6: Dismissal and Notice of Rights.

Document 7A: Notice of Right to Sue, issued on request 180 days after filing of initial charge.

Document 7B: Notice of Right to Sue, issued after an EEOC investigation. (This is typically used only when claimant does not hire an attorney, and in class action suits.)

chment to EEOC Form 161,
-A, or 161-B (Rev. 3/98)

INFORMATION RELATED TO FILING SUIT
UNDER THE LAWS ENFORCED BY THE EEOC

(This information relates to filing suit in Federal or State court under Federal law.
If you also plan to sue claiming violations of State law, please be aware that time limits and other
provisions of State law may be shorter or more limited than those described below.)

RIVATE SUIT RIGHTS -- **Title VII of the Civil Rights Act, the Americans with Disabilities Act (ADA), or the Age Discrimination in Employment Act (ADEA):**

 order to pursue this matter further, you must file a lawsuit against the respondent(s) named in the charge **ithin 90 days** of the date you *receive* this Notice. Therefore, you should **keep a record of this date**. Once is 90-day period is over, your right to sue based on the charge referred to in this Notice will be lost. If you tend to consult an attorney, you should do so promptly. Give your attorney a copy of this Notice, and its velope, and tell him or her the date you received it. Furthermore, in order to avoid any question that you d not act in a timely manner, it is prudent that your suit be filed **within 90 days of the date this Notice was ailed** to you (as indicated where the Notice is signed) or the date of the postmark, if later.

our lawsuit may be filed in U.S. District Court or a State court of competent jurisdiction. (Usually, the propriate State court is the general civil trial court.) Whether you file in Federal or State court is a matter r you to decide after talking to your attorney. Filing this Notice is not enough. You must file a "complaint" at contains a short statement of the facts of your case which shows that you are entitled to relief. Your suit ay include any matter alleged in the charge or, to the extent permitted by court decisions, matters like or lated to the matters alleged in the charge. Generally, suits are brought in the State where the alleged lawful practice occurred, but in some cases can be brought where relevant employment records are kept, here the employment would have been, or where the respondent has its main office. If you have simple lestions, you usually can get answers from the office of the clerk of the court where you are bringing suit, at do not expect that office to write your complaint or make legal strategy decisions for you.

RIVATE SUIT RIGHTS -- Equal Pay Act (EPA):

PA suits must be filed in court within 2 years (3 years for willful violations) of the alleged EPA derpayment: backpay due for violations that occurred **more than 2 years (3 years)** before you file suit may t be collectible. For example, if you were underpaid under the EPA for work performed from 7/1/97 to /1/97, you should file suit **before 7/1/99** -- *not* 12/1/99 -- in order to recover unpaid wages due for July 97. This time limit for filing an EPA suit is separate from the 90-day filing period under Title VII, the ADA the ADEA referred to above. Therefore, if you also plan to sue under Title VII, the ADA or the ADEA, addition to suing on the EPA claim, suit must be filed within 90 days of this Notice and within the 2- or 3- ar EPA back pay recovery period.

TTORNEY REPRESENTATION -- Title VII and the ADA:

 you cannot afford or have been unable to obtain a lawyer to represent you, the U.S. District Court having risdiction in your case may, in limited circumstances, assist you in obtaining a lawyer. Requests for help ust be made to the U.S. District Court in the form and manner it requires (you should be prepared to explain detail your efforts to retain an attorney). Requests should be made well before the end of the 90-day period ntioned above, because such requests do not relieve you of the requirement to bring suit within 90 days.

TTORNEY REFERRAL AND EEOC ASSISTANCE -- All Statutes:

ou may contact the EEOC representative shown on your Notice if you need help in finding a lawyer or if you ve any questions about your legal rights, including advice on which U.S. District Court can hear your case. you need to inspect or obtain a copy of information in EEOC's file on the charge, please request it promptly writing and provide your charge number (as shown on your Notice). While EEOC destroys charge files ter a certain time, all charge files are kept for at least 6 months after our last action on the case. Therefore, you file suit and want to review the charge file, **please make your review request within 6 months** of this otice. (Before filing suit, any request should be made within the next 90 days.)

IF YOU FILE SUIT, PLEASE SEND A COPY OF YOUR COURT COMPLAINT TO THIS OFFICE.

Document 2

CHARGE QUESTIONNAIRE

| | EEOC Use Only | Name (Intake Officer) |

This form is affected by the Privacy Act of 1974; see Privacy Act Statement on back before completing this form.

Please answer the following questions, telling us briefly why you believe you have been discriminated against in employment. An officer of the EEOC will talk with you after you complete this form.

Social Security Number _____ - ____ - _____

(Please Print)

NAME _____ DATE _____

(First)   (Middle Name or Initial)   (Last)

ADDRESS _____ TELEPHONE NO. (Include area code) _____

CITY _____ STATE _____ ZIP _____ COUNTY _____

Please provide the name of an individual at a different address in your local area who would know how to reach you.

NAME _____ RELATIONSHIP _____ PHONE _____

ADDRESS _____ CITY _____ STATE _____ ZIP _____

I believe I was discriminated against by: (Check those that apply)

☐ EMPLOYER   ☐ UNION (Give Local No.)   ☐ EMPLOYMENT AGENCY   ☐ OTHER (Specify)

APPROX NO. EMPLOYED BY THIS EMPLOYER _____

NAME _____	NAME _____
ADDRESS _____	ADDRESS _____
_____	_____
CITY, STATE, ZIP _____	CITY, STATE, ZIP _____

If you checked "Employer" above, are you now employed by the Employer that you believed discriminated against you?

YES: From _____   NO: I applied for _____   OR: I was employed as _____
      (date)   (position)   (position)

                              on _____   until _____ . I was was _____
(current position)   (date)   (date)   (laid off, fired, etc.)

What action was taken against you that you believe to be discriminatory? What harm, if any, was caused to you or others in your work situation as a result of that action? (if more space is required, use reverse.)

_____

_____

_____

_____

_____

_____

_____

_____

_____

_____

WHAT WAS THE MOST RECENT DATE THE HARM YOU ALLEGED TOOK PLACE? _____

EEOC Form 283 (12/93)   (Previous editions of this form are obsolete and should not be used.)

Document 2 (cont'd.)

Why do you believe this action was taken against you?

_____

_____

_____

_____

_____

_____

_____

_____

_____

_____

_____

_____

_____

Normally, your identity as a complainant will be disclosed to the organization which allegedly discriminated against you.

Do you [   ] consent or [   ] not consent to such disclosures?

Have you sought assistance about the action you think was discriminatory from any agency, from your union, an attorney, or from any other source? [   ] No [   ] Yes (If answer is yes, complete below.)

NAME OF SOURCE ASSISTANCE _____ DATE _____

RESULTS IF ANY: _____

Have you filed a complaint about the action you think was discriminatory with any other Federal, State, or Local Government Anti-discrimination agency? [   ] No [   ] Yes (If answer is yes, complete below.)

NAME OF SOURCE ASSISTANCE _____ DATE _____

RESULTS IF ANY: _____

Have you filed an EEOC Charge in the past? [   ] No [   ] Yes (if answer is yes, complete below)

APPROX. DATE FILED	ORGANIZATION CHARGED	CHARGE NUMBER (IF KNOWN)

I declare under penalty of perjury that the foregoing is true and correct.

SIGNATURE   DATE

PRIVACY ACT STATEMENT: This form is covered by the Privacy Act of 1974: Public Law 93-579. Authority for requesting personal data and the uses thereof are:

1. **FORM NUMBER/TITLE/DATE.** EEOC Form 283, Charge Questionnaire (12/93).

2. **AUTHORITY.** 42 U.S.C. § 2000e-5(b), 29 U.S.C. § 211, 29 U.S.C. § 626. 42 U.S.C. 12117(a)

3. **PRINCIPAL PURPOSE.** The purpose of this questionnaire is to solicit information in an acceptable form consistent with statutory requirements to enable the Commission to act on matters within its jurisdiction. When this form constitutes the only timely written statement of allegations of employment discrimination, the Commission will, consistent with 29 CFR 1601.12(b) and 29 CFR 1626.8(b), consider it to be a sufficient charge of discrimination under the relevant statute(s).

4. **ROUTINE USES.** Information provided on this form will be used by Commission employees to determine the existence of facts relevant to a decision as to whether the Commission has jurisdiction over allegations of employment discrimination and to provide such charge filing counselling as is appropriate. Information provided on this form may be disclosed to other State, local and federal agencies as may be appropriate or necessary to carrying out the Commission's functions. Information may also be disclosed to charging parties in consideration of or in connection with litigation.

5. **WHETHER DISCLOSURE IS MANDATORY OR VOLUNTARY AND EFFECT ON INDIVIDUAL FOR NOT PROVIDING INFORMATION.** The providing of this information is voluntary but the failure to do so may hamper the Commission's investigation of a charge of discrimination. It is not mandatory that this form be used to provide the requested information.

Reverse Side of Form 283

Document 3

CHARGE OF DISCRIMINATION

This form is affected by the Privacy Act of 1974; See Privacy Act Statement before completing this form.

AGENCY	CHARGE NUMBER
☐ FEPA	
☐ EEOC	

_____ and EEOC

State or local Agency, if any

NAME (Indicate Mr., Ms., Mrs.)	HOME TELEPHONE (Include Area Code)

STREET ADDRESS	CITY, STATE AND ZIP CODE	DATE OF BIRTH

NAMED IS THE EMPLOYER, LABOR ORGANIZATION, EMPLOYMENT AGENCY, APPRENTICESHIP COMMITTEE, STATE OR LOCAL GOVERNMENT AGENCY WHO DISCRIMINATED AGAINST ME (If more than one list below.)

NAME	NUMBER OF EMPLOYEES, MEMBERS	TELEPHONE (Include Area Code)

STREET ADDRESS	CITY, STATE AND ZIP CODE	COUNTY

NAME	TELEPHONE NUMBER (Include Area Code)

STREET ADDRESS	CITY, STATE AND ZIP CODE	COUNTY

CAUSE OF DISCRIMINATION BASED ON (Check appropriate box(es))

☐ RACE ☐ COLOR ☐ SEX ☐ RELIGION ☐ AGE
☐ RETALIATION ☐ NATIONAL ORIGIN ☐ DISABILITY ☐ OTHER (Specify)

DATE DISCRIMINATION TOOK PLACE
EARLIEST (ADEA/EPA)   LATEST (ALL)

☐ CONTINUING ACTION

THE PARTICULARS ARE (If additional paper is needed, attach extra sheet(s)):

I want this charge filed with both the EEOC and the State or local Agency, if any. I will advise the agencies if I change my address or telephone number and I will cooperate fully with them in the processing of my charge in accordance with their proceedures.

I delcare under penalty of perjury that the foregoing is true and correct.

Date _____ Charging Party (Signature)

NOTARY - (When necessary for State and Local Requirements)

I swear or affirm that I have read the above charge and that it is true to the best of my knowledge, information and belief.

SIGNATURE OF COMPLAINANT

SUBSCRIBED AND SWORN TO BEFORE ME THIS DATE
(Day, month, and year)

EEOC FORM 5 (Rev. 12/93)

(FIELD OFFICE LETTERHEAD)

Respondent:
Charge No.:

ar   :

is is to acknowledge your charge of employment discrimination against the above named respondent. The formation you have provided indicates that your charge is subject to [Title VII of the Civil Rights Act (Title I); the Age Discrimination in Employment Act (ADEA); the Equal Pay Act (EPA); and/or the Americans th Disabilities Act (ADA)].

u need do nothing further at this time. We will contact you when we need further information or sistance. A copy or notice of your charge will be provided to the respondent as required by our procedures. ease refer to the charge number above whenever you contact us about your charge.

e Commission's regulations require that you notify this office of any change in address and keep us formed of any prolonged absence from your current address. Your failure to cooperate in this matter may d to dismissal of your charge.

TION PARAGRAPH FOR DEFERRAL JURISDICTIONS

ou should be aware that the Commission will provide a copy of your charge to the (state or local agency) accordance with our procedures. If your charge is investigated by that agency, you may be required to ear to or affirm your signature before a notary public or an official of that agency].

TION PARAGRAPH FOR DEFERRAL JURISDICTION - CERTIFIED AGENCIES

your charge is investigated by that agency, they will investigate and resolve your charge under their statute. der Section 1601.76 of EEOC's regulations, you are entitled to request that EEOC perform a Substantial eight Review of the agency's final finding. To secure this review, you must request it in writing to this ice within 15 days of your receipt of the agency's final finding in your case. Otherwise, we will generally opt the agency's finding as EEOC's.]

Sincerely,

Commission Representative

closure
Charging Party Information Sheet

(REPLY TO CORRESPONDENCE WHICH IS A COMPLETED CHARGE)

Exhibit 2-B

Document 5

(FIELD OFFICE LETTERHEAD)

Charge Number:
Charging Party: [Do not name charging party if
                s/he is not named on Form 131/131-A or
                when s/he has requested confidentiality.]

Dear   :

This is to inform you that the charge cited above **[has been withdrawn as a result of a negotiated settlement between you and the charging party (or) has been withdrawn as the result of a request from the charging party]** pursuant to the Commission's regulations under Title VII, the ADA, and the ADEA.

1. [ ] While the Commission has accepted this withdrawal, it will continue its investigation of your organization under the **[ADEA, pursuant to § 1626.4 of the ADEA regulations/EPA, pursuant to § 1620.19 of the EPA regulations]**.

2. [ ] The Commission has informed the **[FEPA]** of this withdrawal. Any questions you may have regarding further action by that agency should be addressed directly to it.

3. [ ] The Commission's acceptance of this withdrawal terminates the investigation of this charge. This withdrawal does not affect the investigation of any other charge.

On behalf of the Commission:

_____

(NOTICE TO RESPONDENT OF WITHDRAWAL OF CHARGE WHEN
RESPONDENT HAS RECEIVED NOTICE OF CHARGE)

Exhibit 7-D

Document 6

OC Form 161 (3/98)

U.S. EQUAL EMPLOYMENT OPPORTUNITY COMMISSION

DISMISSAL AND NOTICE OF RIGHTS

To:	From:

[ ] *On behalf of person(s) aggrieved whose identity is*
   CONFIDENTIAL (29 CFR § 1601.7(a))

harge No.	EEOC Representative	Telephone No.

HE EEOC IS CLOSING ITS FILE ON THIS CHARGE FOR THE FOLLOWING REASON:

] The facts alleged in the charge fail to state a claim under any of the statutes enforced by the EEOC.

] Your allegations did not involve a disability as defined by the Americans with Disabilities Act.

] The Respondent employs less than the required number of employees or is not otherwise covered by the statutes.

] Your charge was not timely filed with the Commission; in other words, you waited too long after the date(s) of the alleged discrimination to file your charge.

] You were given 30 days in which to respond, but failed to provide information, failed to appear or be available for interviews/conferences, or otherwise failed to cooperate to the extent that it was not possible to resolve your charge.

] While reasonable efforts were made to locate you, we were not able to do so.

] You were given 30 days to accept a reasonable settlement offer that affords full relief for the harm you alleged.

] The EEOC issues the following determination: Based upon its investigation, the EEOC is unable to conclude that the information obtained establishes violations of the statutes. This does not certify that the respondent is in compliance with the statutes. No finding is made as to any other issues that might be construed as having been raised by this charge.

] The EEOC has adopted the findings of the state or local fair employment practices agency that investigated this charge.

] Other *(briefly state)* _____

-- NOTICE OF SUIT RIGHTS --
(See the additional information attached to this form.)

le VII, Americans with Disabilities Act, and/or Age Discrimination in Employment Act: This will be the only notice of missal and of your right to sue that we will send you. You may file a lawsuit against the respondent(s) under federal law based this charge in federal or state court. Your lawsuit **must be filed WITHIN 90 DAYS of your receipt of this Notice**, or your right sue based on this charge will be lost. (The time limit for filing suit based on a claim under state law may be different.)

qual Pay Act (EPA): EPA suits must be filed in federal or state court within 2 years (3 years for willful violations) of the alleged A underpayment. This means that **backpay due for any violations that occurred more than 2 years (3 years)** before you file t may not be collectible.

On behalf of the Commission

closure(s)

_____   _____
                                       (Date Mailed)

Document 7A

EEOC Form 161-B (3/98)

U. S. EQUAL EMPLOYMENT OPPORTUNITY COMMISSION

NOTICE OF RIGHT TO SUE *(ISSUED ON REQUEST)*

To:	From:

[ ] *On behalf of person(s) aggrieved whose identity is*
      CONFIDENTIAL (29 CFR § 1601.7(a))

Charge No.	EEOC Representative	Telephone No.

NOTICE TO THE PERSON AGGRIEVED: *(See also the additional information attached to this for*

Title VII of the Civil Rights Act of 1964 and/or the Americans with Disabilities Act (ADA): This is your Notice of Right to S issued under Title VII and/or the ADA based on the above-numbered charge. It has been issued at your request. Your lawsuit un Title VII or the ADA **must be filed in federal or state court <u>WITHIN 90 DAYS</u> of your receipt of this Notice,** or your righ sue based on this charge will be lost. (The time limit for filing suit based on a claim under state law may be different.)

[ ]   More than 180 days have passed since the filing of this charge.

[ ]   Less than 180 days have passed since the filing of this charge, but I have determined that it is unlikely that the EEOC be able to complete its administrative processing within 180 days from the filing of the charge.

[ ]   The EEOC is terminating its processing of this charge.

[ ]   The EEOC will continue to process this charge.

Age Discrimination in Employment Act (ADEA): You may sue under the ADEA at any time from 60 days after the charge filed until 90 days after you receive notice that we have completed action on the charge. In this regard, **the paragraph mar below applies to your case:**

[ ]   The EEOC is closing your case. Therefore, your lawsuit under the ADEA **must be filed in federal or state court <u>WITH</u> <u>90 DAYS</u> of your receipt of this Notice.** Otherwise, your right to sue based on the above-numbered charge will be l

[ ]   The EEOC is continuing its handling of your ADEA case. However, if 60 days have passed since the filing of your cha you may file suit in federal or state court under the ADEA at this time.

Equal Pay Act (EPA): You already have the right to sue under the EPA (filing an EEOC charge is not required). EPA suits m be brought in federal or state court within 2 years (3 years for willful violations) of the alleged EPA underpayment. This means **backpay due for any violations that occurred <u>more than 2 years (3 years)</u> before you file suit may not be collectible.**

If you file suit based on this charge, please send a copy of your court complaint to this office.

On behalf of the Commission

Enclosure(s)   *(Date Mailed)*

cc:

Document 7B

EEOC Form 161-A (3/98)   **U. S. EQUAL EMPLOYMENT OPPORTUNITY COMMISSION**

NOTICE OF RIGHT TO SUE
(CONCILIATION FAILURE)

To:	From:

[   ] *On behalf of person(s) aggrieved whose identity is*
       CONFIDENTIAL (29 CFR § 1601.7(a))

Charge No.	EEOC Representative	Telephone No.

TO THE PERSON AGGRIEVED:

This Notice concludes the EEOC's processing of the above-numbered charge. The EEOC found reasonable cause to believe that violations of the statute(s) occurred with respect to some or all of the matters alleged in the charge but could not obtain a settlement with the Respondent that would provide relief for you. In addition, the EEOC has decided that it will not bring suit against the Respondent at this time based on this charge and will close its file in this case. This does not mean that the EEOC is certifying that the Respondent is in compliance with the law, or that the EEOC will not sue the Respondent later or intervene later in your lawsuit if you decide to sue on your own behalf.

-- NOTICE OF SUIT RIGHTS --
(See the additional information attached to this form.)

Title VII, Americans with Disabilities Act, and/or Age Discrimination in Employment Act: This will be the only notice of your right to sue that we will send you. You may file a lawsuit against the respondent(s) under federal law based on this charge in federal or state court. Your lawsuit **must be filed <u>WITHIN 90 DAYS</u> from your receipt of this Notice,** or your right to sue based on this charge will be lost. (The time limit for filing suit based on a claim under state law may be different.)

Equal Pay Act (EPA): EPA suits must be brought in federal or state court within 2 years (3 years for willful violations) of the alleged EPA underpayment. This means that **backpay due for any violations that occurred <u>more than 2 years (3 years)</u>** before you file suit may not be collectible.

If you file suit based on this charge, please send a copy of your court complaint to this office.

On behalf of the Commission

Enclosure(s)   _____   _____

                                                                     (Date Mailed)

c:

INDEX